Steroids and Performance Drugs

INVESTIGATE

SARA L. LATTA

Enslow Publishers, Inc.
40 Industrial Road
Box 398
Berkeley Heights, NJ 07922
USA

http://www.enslow.com

Copyright © 2015 by Sara L. Latta

All rights reserved.

No part of this book may be reproduced by any means without the written permission of the publisher.

Library of Congress Cataloging-in-Publication Data

Latta, Sara L.
 Investigate steroids and performance drugs / Sara Latta.
   pages cm — (Investigate drugs)
  Summary: "Find out about the history of steroids and other performance-enhancing drugs, how they work, their effects, and why people use and abuse them"— Provided by publisher.
  Includes bibliographical references and index.
  ISBN 978-0-7660-4240-7
 1. Steroid abuse—Juvenile literature. 2. Steroid abuse—History—Juvenile literature. 3. Steroids—Physiological effect—Juvenile literature. I. Title.
 HV5822.S68L38 2015
 362.29'9—dc23
                               2013028820

Future editions:
Paperback ISBN: 978-1-4644-0423-8   EPUB ISBN: 978-1-4645-1231-5
Single-User PDF ISBN: 978-1-4646-1231-2   Multi-User PDF ISBN: 978-0-7660-5863-7

Printed in the United States of America

052014 Lake Book Manufacturing, Inc., Melrose Park, IL

10 9 8 7 6 5 4 3 2 1

To Our Readers: We have done our best to make sure all Internet Addresses in this book were active and appropriate when we went to press. However, the author and the publisher have no control over and assume no liability for the material available on those Internet sites or on other Web sites they may link to. Any comments or suggestions can be sent by e-mail to comments@enslow.com or to the address on the back cover. Enslow Publishers, Inc., is committed to printing our books on recycled paper. The paper in every book contains 10% to 30% post-consumer waste (PCW).

♻ Enslow Publishers, Inc., is committed to printing our books on recycled paper. The paper in every book contains 10% to 30% post-consumer waste (PCW). The cover board on the outside of each book contains 100% PCW. Our goal is to do our part to help young people and the environment too!

Photo Credits: © 2013 Thinkstock: Aleksandar Todorovic/iStock, p. 47; allanswart/iStock, p. 13; AustralisPhotography/ iStock, p. 44; Ben Ryan/iStock, p. 31; diego cervo/iStock, p. 76; Digital Vision, pp. 25, 57; Dorling Kindersley RF pp. 16 (top), 43, 64; Dynamic Graphics/liquidlibrary, p. 66; Jana Blašková/iStock, p. 56; Joe Norman/iStock, p. 34; JupiterImages/Photos.com, pp. 18, 29, 76; Matthew Scherf/iStock, p. 85; Nancy Brammer/iStock, p. 7; nyul/iStock, p. 90; Spike Mafford/PhotoDisc, p. 39; Steven Wynn/iStock: p. 16 (bottom); william howe/iStockp. 11; Yuri Minaev/iStock, p. 22; AP Photo/Kathy Willens, p. 40; Associated Press/ Dieter Endlicher, p. 27; National Archives, p. 21; Shutterstock.com: Arlens, pp. 1 (photo effect), 3-4, 5, 15, 33, 50, 61, 74, 83; Jan Mika, p. 36; antoshkaforever, pp.48, 60; PhotostockAR, p. 59; fotostokers, pp. 62, 72; Stanley B. Burns, MD and The Burns Archive, p. 19; Wikipedia.com Public Domain Image, pp. 52, 79.

Cover Illustration: Jupiter Images/liquidlibrary/© 2013 Thinkstock

Chapter 1	**PERFORMANCE** *Drugs*	5
Chapter 2	**HISTORY OF** *Steroids and Performance-enhancing Drugs*	15
Chapter 3	**MUSCLE BUILDERS:** *Anabolic Androgenic Steroids, Steroid Precursors, and Other Hormones*	33
Chapter 4	**OXYGEN BOOSTERS:** *EPO and Blood Doping*	50

Chapter 5 — SPEED IT UP; SLOW IT DOWN: Stimulants and Relaxants — 61

Chapter 6 — SOMETHING ON THE SIDE: Creatine and Other Supplements — 74

Chapter 7 — DIURETICS and Masking Agents — 83

Chapter Notes 92
Getting Help 97
Glossary 98
For More Information 100
Further Reading 101
Index 102

Chapter 1

PERFORMANCE Drugs

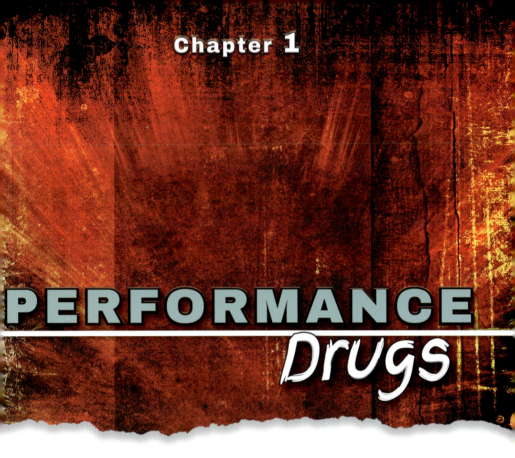

Taylor Hooton might have followed his cousin Burt Hooton, a pitcher who once threw a no-hitter for the Chicago Cubs, into the majors. He had a good arm, and as a junior at West Plano High School in Texas, he had a shot at making the varsity baseball team the next season. He was also popular and good-looking. Like many teens, his looks were very important to him. At 6 feet 2 inches and about 175 pounds, he was lean and strong, but he didn't have the muscular build he wanted. In the fall of his junior year, one of his coaches told him that he needed to get bigger if he wanted to pitch varsity. That sealed the deal, as far as Taylor was concerned. He knew that he could get bigger by spending more time in the weight room and changing his eating habits, but it would take hard work and time. He knew a lot

INVESTIGATE STEROIDS AND PERFORMANCE DRUGS

of other kids at school who had used steroids, and they'd gained a lot of muscle, fast. It was no secret that some guys in the major leagues juiced, and they had the home run records to show for it. As far as he could tell, there were no side effects—as long as he didn't get caught.

In February, Taylor began buying steroids with money he'd stolen from his mother—something he'd never done before. In a matter of weeks, he was considerably bigger and stronger. However, he also developed a severe case of acne on his back (a common side effect of steroid use). Worse, he became increasingly angry and irritable. His girlfriend, Emily, recalled violent mood swings; little things would cause him to fly off the handle, punching walls and doors until his hands bled. In an interview with CBS News, his mother said that "[he] went from a calm person, like we're talking now, to these rages, yelling and screaming, and hittin' on the table, and stompin' out of the room. Totally un-Taylor like." Later, he would apologize for his outbursts, but they happened again and again.[1]

Taylor's parents began to suspect that their son was using steroids. They sent him to a psychiatrist, who found that he was suffering from major depression. She suspected that the anabolic steroids he admitted using were at least partly to blame. She told Taylor to quit taking the steroids and put him on a drug to help him with his depression. He quit the steroids, but his depression just got worse (a common reaction to withdrawal from the drugs). That summer, following a family vacation, his parents discovered that he had stolen a digital camera and laptop computer—probably so that he could sell them to buy more steroids. The next

Athletes, even those in high school, sometimes feel the pressure to take drugs to get bigger and stronger.

INVESTIGATE STEROIDS AND PERFORMANCE DRUGS

day, he used two belts to make a noose and hanged himself in his bedroom.

Later, Taylor's father discovered vials of steroids, needles, and syringes in his room. Doctors examining Taylor's body found that he had begun using steroids again. Taylor's parents and doctors are certain that his suicide was a direct result of his steroid use. "He's gone. And it's devastating," Taylor's father told CBS News. "We'll never get over it."[2]

Taylor Hooton's story may be an extreme one, but it's a sobering example of just how dangerous steroids and other performance-enhancing drugs can be. Despite the risks, more and more teens who want to gain an edge on the playing field, battle fatigue, or simply look better are experimenting with these substances. Some performance-enhancing drugs can even hide the use of other illegal substances. A study from the University of Minnesota found that among middle school and high school teens in the Minneapolis-St. Paul area, nearly 6 percent of boys and 4.6 percent of girls reported using anabolic steroids.[3]

It can be difficult to stay clean when it seems that so many people are using performance-enhancing drugs, but you should keep a couple of things in mind. First, it's cheating. Cheating is the same as a lie, and cheaters often get caught. Look at cyclist Lance Armstrong, who was stripped of his Tour de France titles and is now banned from all professional sports. Second, these drugs cause serious physical and mental disorders, even death. Many performance-enhancing drugs are especially dangerous for teens, whose bodies and brains are still developing.

PERFORMANCE *DRUGS*

Drugs like anabolic steroids that increase muscle mass and strength are among the most commonly abused performance-enhancing drugs. But you could fill whole medicine cabinets with other kinds of performance-enhancing drugs. Here is a quick overview of these drugs; we'll take a closer look in the chapters to follow.

Muscle Builders

Anabolic androgenic steroids—that's a real mouthful. No wonder most people just called them steroids, even though there are many different kinds of these compounds. These particular drugs are "anabolic" because they build muscle. They are "androgenic" because they are associated with male characteristics, such as deep voice or increased hair growth. And they are "steroids" because they are a type of hormone. Anabolic androgenic steroids (AAS) are essentially artificially produced versions of testosterone, the male sex hormone. There are some legitimate medical reasons for using AAS. Doctors may prescribe them under close supervision for people who don't produce enough testosterone on their own, or have certain blood disorders or types of cancer. But doctors cannot legally prescribe anabolic steroids for the sole purpose of building muscles, as they can be harmful in otherwise healthy people. They are currently banned by most sports organizations, including the International Olympic Committee, the National Football League, the National Basketball Association, the National Collegiate Athletic Association, the National Hockey League, and Major League Baseball.

INVESTIGATE STEROIDS AND
PERFORMANCE DRUGS

Some supplements contain anabolic steroid precursors, or prohormones. These are substances that the body can convert into steroids. Like AAS, most are illegal without a doctor's prescription.

Other substances that athletes sometimes take to boost their muscle growth include human growth hormone (hGH), human chorionic gonadotropin (hCG), luteinizing hormone (LH), and insulin-like growth factors. These drugs are only approved for athletes who have illnesses or conditions that are treated by the drugs.

Oxygen Boosters

Some athletes, like those who need a lot of endurance—cyclists and long-distance runners, for example—don't need bigger or stronger muscles. They need to be able to increase their body's ability to deliver oxygen to the muscles over long periods of time. Athletes can condition their bodies to hold and deliver greater amounts of oxygen through proper training. Oxygen is carried through the blood by red blood cells, so some athletes try to get the edge by increasing the amount of red blood cells in the body.

One approach is blood doping. An athlete removes some of his or her own blood (just as he or she would do when donating blood), stores it until the body has had time to replace it, and then injects it back in shortly before the race. Voila—more red blood cells! Others use a synthetic form of a hormone made by the body, erythropoietin (EPO). EPO stimulates the bone marrow to make more red blood cells. Blood doping and EPO are both illegal for use in athletic events. They are also dangerous.

Stimulants

Any athlete knows that being on your game requires a great deal of energy and focus. Athletes (and others) have long used stimulants to help beat fatigue and increase energy and alertness. The caffeine in coffee, some sodas, and energy drinks is a legal stimulant, but some athletes turn to more potent substances, such as amphetamines and ephedra. In recent years, people both on and off the playing field have begun to abuse the stimulant-type drugs used to treat Attention Deficit Hyperactivity Disorder (ADHD). While stimulants can temporarily increase athletic performance, they are quite addictive, can have serious side effects, and cannot be prescribed by physicians for this purpose.

Something on the Side: Creatine and Other Supplements

Many athletes do take nutritional supplements, which are very easy to buy over the counter. Although supplements are not illegal, they may still be risky. Because supplements are not considered either a food or a drug, they are not regulated by the Food and Drug Administration.

INVESTIGATE STEROIDS AND
PERFORMANCE DRUGS

There is no guarantee that supplements actually contain the ingredients listed on the labels, or whether they actually deliver the benefits the makers claim. Supplements have been found to be contaminated with banned performance-enhancing drugs (including steroids), so they may lead to positive drug tests.

One of the most popular supplements among athletes is creatine, which helps muscles release energy. Your liver

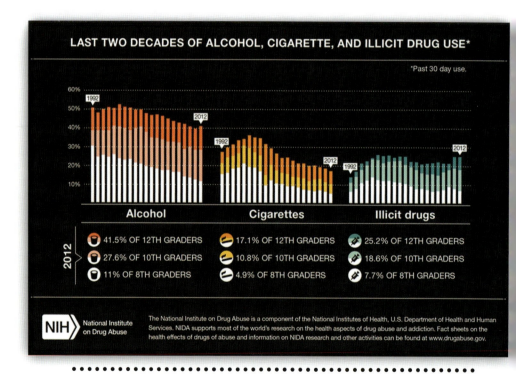

This chart from the National Institute of Drug Abuse tracks two decades (1992-2012) of alcohol, cigarette, and illicit drug use by eighth-, tenth-, and twelfth-grade students.

PERFORMANCE *DRUGS*

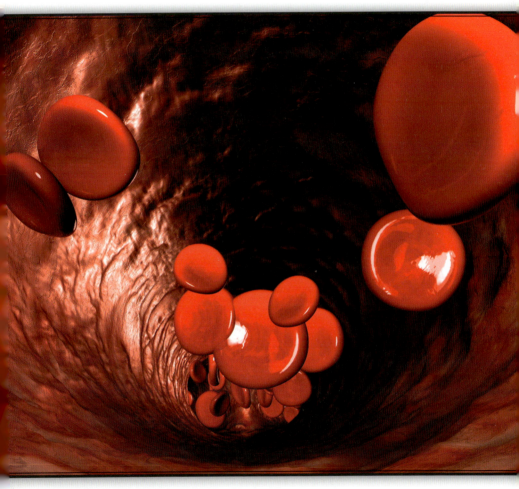

Athletes who engage in illegal blood doping aim to have more red blood cells to carry oxygen in their blood.

INVESTIGATE STEROIDS AND PERFORMANCE DRUGS

makes small amounts each day, and if you're a meat eater, you get it in your diet as well.

Weight Loss and Deception

Some athletes—wrestlers, jockeys, and boxers, among others—have to meet certain weight requirements. If they are a little over their desired weight, they sometimes take a drug called a diuretic. It causes them to urinate more than usual, so they lose water weight. Athletes who abuse other drugs sometimes take diuretics or other masking agents to help them pass drug tests. These drugs make it more difficult to detect any illegal drugs. Like other PEDs, diuretics can be dangerous, even deadly.

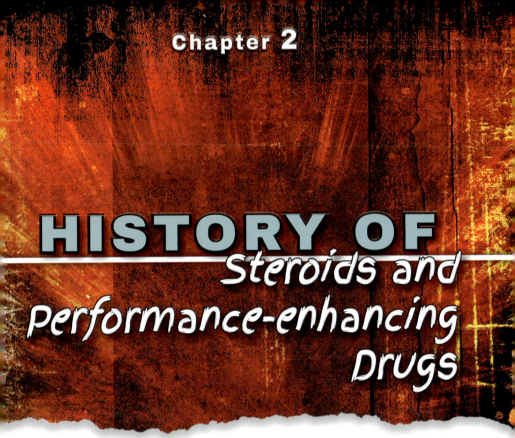

Chapter 2

HISTORY OF Steroids and Performance-enhancing Drugs

It's probably safe to say that athletes have been using performance-enhancing drugs as long as there have been sporting events. Certainly we know that athletes in the original Olympic Games (held every four years from 776 B.C. to A.D. 394) tried different diets and drugs to improve their performance. One winning athlete relied upon a special diet of dried figs; another swore by a meat-heavy diet (this was a time when people didn't eat that much meat). They also ate mushrooms that caused hallucinations and drank a variety of stimulating potions.

Galen, a Greek physician, is said to have prescribed "the rear hooves of an Abyssinian [donkey], ground up, boiled in oil, and flavoured with rosehips and rose petals" to improve an athlete's performance.[1] Long before anybody knew about

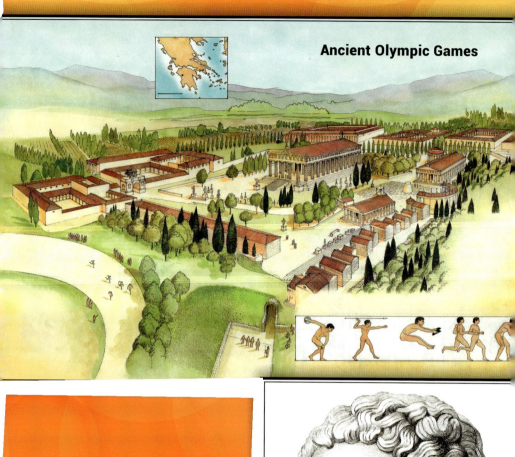

Ancient Olympic Games

antique bust of Galen,

HISTORY OF *STEROIDS AND PERFORMANCE-ENHANCING DRUGS*

the male hormone testosterone, athletes ate the testicles of bulls and sheep, believing that they would make them stronger and more aggressive. There were cheaters in the ancient Olympics, just as there are today, but they were more likely to be caught trying to bribe officials or losing a match on purpose for money. The ancient Greeks didn't seem to consider the use of drugs cheating.

In fact, performance-enhancing drugs seemed to be an accepted fact of life in many ancient cultures. Ancient Roman gladiators drank a potion laced with strychnine (a stimulant that can be deadly in higher doses) to ward off fatigue. West African runners chewed the caffeine-rich kola nut before races, and the people of Peru living in the Andes chewed coca leaves (which contain small amounts of cocaine) to improve their endurance. Ancient Norse warriors called Berserkers used a drug made from a mushroom that made them fight with a crazed fury—so when we say someone has "gone berserk," we mean they're in a wild rage.[2]

The Modern Era of Doping

Fast forward to 1896. By this time, swimmers, runners, cyclists, and other athletes used stimulants in races in much the same way that today's athletes guzzle sports drinks. Bicycle and foot races lasting six days and nights were all the rage, so perhaps it was no surprise that athletes would do just about anything to keep themselves going the distance. Since everyone used drugs, the trick was to find some "magic potion" that would give an athlete an edge over the competition. Their choice of stimulants ranged

Lethal games of combat between gladiators were popular all over the Roman Empire, where amphitheaters and scenes like this one were widely found.

from the relatively harmless (caffeine) to the definitely dangerous (opium, cocaine, heroin, and strychnine). That year, cyclist Major Taylor, one of the first African-American superstar athletes, took part in a six-day race at New York's Madison Square Garden. He finished eighth after suffering from hallucinations, fueled by exhaustion and drugs. At one point he said, "I cannot go on with safety, for there is a man chasing me around the ring with a knife in his hand."[3]

In 1904, Thomas Hicks nearly died after winning the Olympic marathon in St. Louis, Missouri. The marathon began in the middle of a brutally hot, humid afternoon on a dusty 26.2-mile course. With about ten miles left to go, Hicks asked his support team for water. They gave him a mixture of brandy, strychnine, and raw eggs instead. He was given two more doses of the stuff before collapsing at the finish line. The combination of running in the heat, alcohol, and strychnine nearly killed him. Miraculously, he was on

Cyclist Major Taylor competed in a six-day race at New York's Madison Square Garden. This photo was taken around 1900.

his feet after about an hour, although that was the end of his racing career.

Speed It Up: Amphetamines

In World War II, soldiers took amphetamines to reduce fatigue and increase endurance on the battlefield. American bomber pilots used amphetamines to help them stay awake during long missions. Amphetamines, or "pep pills," became the go-to drug for students pulling all-nighters before a test and athletes wishing to gain an edge on their opponents. And while the pills did indeed boost performance—in the beginning, at any rate—many users found that using speed often led to addiction, injury, or worse.

In 1960, a Danish cyclist named Knud Enemark Jensen became the first Olympic athlete whose death could be directly related to doping. He was racing in a 100-kilometer time trial on a very hot day in Rome. He began to feel ill with about 20 kilometers left to go. Ten kilometers later, he fell off his bike and crashed. Hours later, he died. Although sunstroke was the official cause of death, traces of a stimulant were found in his blood, and his trainer admitted to giving drugs to Jensen and other team members.

Seven years later, British cyclist Tommy Simpson died during an especially brutal leg of the Tour de France. He was cycling up a steep and windy mountain on a very hot day. He had run out of water, so he took a few sips of brandy (we now know that alcohol can cause dehydration, but they didn't know that then). He was two miles from the top of the mountain when he began to weave from side to side. The amphetamines in his system kept him going, though,

World War II bomber pilots sometimes took pep pills to stay awake during long missions. According to the original caption this was the first big raid by the 8th Air Force on a Focke Wulf plant at Marienburg. Coming back, the Germans were up in full force and we lost at least 80 ships - 800 men, many of them pals, 1943, Army Air Forces.

INVESTIGATE STEROIDS AND PERFORMANCE DRUGS

The International Olympic Committee (IOC) banned the use of performance-enhancing drugs in 1967.

even as his body was telling him to stop. A mile later, he collapsed. The man who was probably Britain's greatest cyclist died a short time later.

Although the international governing body for track and field had banned doping by athletes way back in 1928, it wasn't until 1967—shortly before Tommy Simpson's death—that the International Olympic Committee (IOC) banned the use of performance-enhancing drugs. Its initial list of banned drugs was short and limited to stimulants, certain painkillers, and a few others. Athletes were tested for banned substances for the first time at the 1968 Winter Olympic Games.

But anabolic steroids were not on the IOC's list of banned drugs—even though many people suspected that athletes were using them. There was no reliable way of testing for them. Scientists weren't even sure what levels of steroids in an athlete's body could be considered normal. That would soon change.

Pump It Up:
Steroids and Human Growth Hormone

The steroid story began in 1926, with two scientists and forty pounds of bull testicles. The scientists were able to isolate a tiny amount of the male sex hormone, later called testosterone. They injected it into roosters that had been neutered (their testicles had been removed). Soon, the neutered roosters began to cock-a-doodle-doo and strut around just like normal roosters. A few years later, they injected the hormone into men who had been born with little or no testosterone. They, too, developed male characteristics: Their voices deepened, they grew facial hair, and their muscles became bigger and stronger, among other things.

By 1935, German scientists found a way to make testosterone in the lab. Medical doctors began to use it to treat other men whose bodies didn't make enough testosterone. Athletes—even those with normal testosterone levels—

INVESTIGATE STEROIDS AND
PERFORMANCE DRUGS

reasoned that using steroids might help them become stronger and more powerful, too.

Steroids in sports really took off in the 1950s. At the 1954 World Weightlifting Championships in Vienna, Austria, John Ziegler, the doctor for the U.S. team, was astonished by the size and power of the Soviet weightlifters. The Soviet team doctor revealed his team's secret to Ziegler: They were all getting testosterone injections. Once back in the United States, Ziegler, a weightlifter himself, began to experiment with testosterone injections. They made people stronger, all right, but Ziegler worried about the side effects. He developed an anabolic steroid that would have the muscle-building properties of testosterone without the dangerous side effects.

By the 1960s, Ziegler's "mysterious pink pills" were in great demand in the world of weightlifting. Football and baseball soon followed. Former major league pitcher Tom House told a reporter that it was common for baseball players to use performance-enhancing drugs, including steroids, in the late 1960s and early 1970s.[4] To make matters worse, athletes regularly took more than Ziegler recommended. They reasoned that if one pill was good, five would be even better. Ziegler was not happy, because he knew that this was not safe. Ziegler developed heart disease and laid part of the blame on his earlier experiments with testosterone and anabolic steroids. Shortly before his death in 1983, he said that he wished he had never developed the drug, writing, "It is bad enough to have to deal with drug addicts, but now healthy athletes are putting themselves in

Early steroid research involved injecting neutered roosters with testosterone. The neutered roosters started acting just like nonneutered roosters.

INVESTIGATE STEROIDS AND
PERFORMANCE DRUGS

the same category. It's a disgrace. Who plays sports for fun anymore?"[5]

After those early days, the number of athletes using steroids exploded. The first reliable test for anabolic steroid use was developed in 1975. Many sports organizations in the World Anti-Doping Agency, including the IOC, added anabolic steroids to their list of banned substances. Even so, steroid scandals in sports continue to this day.

When British sprinter Ben Johnson set a new world record in the 100-meter race at the Seoul Olympics in 1988, he was stripped of his gold medal after he tested positive for anabolic steroids. By this time, the use of stimulants, steroids, and other performance-enhancing drugs was rampant. One anonymous coach from the Soviet Union said, "I feel sorry for Ben Johnson. All sportsmen—not all, but maybe 90%, including our own—use drugs."[6] While that coach may have been exaggerating, the widespread use of PEDs led some athletes to look for new ways of boosting their performances—and of getting around the drug tests.

Ramp It Up: Blood Doping, EPO, and Synthetic Oxygen Carriers

At 1.5 miles (2,420 meters) above sea level, the air in Mexico City is thin. There is less oxygen available than in places closer to sea level. One of the lessons that athletes learned from the 1968 Olympics in Mexico City is that people who lived, or at least trained, at high altitudes often performed better than those who lived closer to sea level. Their bodies had adapted by increasing the number of red blood cells to carry oxygen to the muscles. This made people realize

Ben Johnson's Olympic gold medal for the 1988 100-meter race in Seoul, Korea, was taken away from him after he tested positive for anabolic steroids.

INVESTIGATE STEROIDS AND
PERFORMANCE DRUGS

that they might be able to boost their performance by giving themselves blood transfusions—their own blood, or that of others with the same blood type. It was—and is—a risky practice, because it could lead to life-threatening blood clots. But it was impossible to detect, especially if an athlete used his or her own blood.

It was widely acknowledged that blood doping was cheating, but it wasn't banned until 1986, after the U.S. cycling team admitted to doing it in the 1984 Olympics in Los Angeles. It wasn't until 2004, though, that scientists developed a reliable test to detect doping using donated blood. The only way to tell whether an athlete is using his or her own blood is to compare blood samples collected at different times; a big increase in the number of red blood cells might indicate doping.

Blood doping became popular, especially among cyclists. But athletes receiving regular blood transfusions ran the risk of becoming infected with bacteria or viruses, or developing life-threatening immune reactions. Athletes began to turn to a new drug, erythropoietin (EPO), that had been developed to treat patients with anemia. A genetically engineered version of a hormone produced by the kidneys, EPO stimulates the body to make more red blood cells. They also turned to synthetic oxygen carriers—chemicals developed in case of emergencies (as on the battlefield) to carry oxygen to the muscles. Reliable tests for EPO and synthetic oxygen carriers would come in 2000 and 2004. Until that time, though, blood doping was common—sometimes with tragic results. Experts believe that at least 20 European cyclists have died as a result of blood doping.

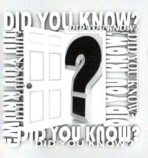

THE INSIDE DOPE
on Testing Race Horses

The first athletes to be tested for drugs were not human—they were horses. Owners or gamblers who had money on a particular horse would hire professional dopers to sneak into the stables and give drugs to their competitor's horses. The drugs did indeed cause the poor animals to run slower—some even died on the racetrack. Many other owners gave their own horses stimulants to make them run faster. This was a problem for the sport of horse racing, but not because the animals suffered (although they did) or some horses had an unfair advantage (which they also did). Instead, it was considered unfair because most of the gamblers who bet on the horses weren't in on the secret. Testing the horses was a way of leveling the playing field—for the gamblers. Although "doping" came to mean using performance-enhancing drugs, "dope" was also slang for information in the horse-racing world. If you were a gambler who had the inside dope on a horse, you knew something that others didn't.

In 1910, chemists developed tests that would detect the most commonly used drugs, cocaine and heroin, in the saliva of horses. It wasn't until the 1930s, though, that racehorses were routinely tested for drugs.

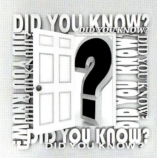

WHAT'S Next?

If the history of sports and performance-enhancing drugs teaches us anything, it's that some athletes and their trainers will do almost anything to win. As more widespread and accurate drug testing makes it more difficult to use anabolic steroids and other PEDs, some experts believe that the future of cheating lies in genetic engineering. That's right: It may soon be possible to change an individual's DNA—the molecule that carries all of the genetic information that makes each person unique—to make him or her bigger, stronger, or faster. This has officials worried, because there may be no test that can detect gene doping.

For example, scientists have created super-muscular mice by shutting off the gene that instructs the cell to make a protein called myostatin. This protein tells muscles when to stop growing. The "Arnold Schwarzenegger mice," as they've become known, bulk up to twice their normal size over a period of weeks because they have no myostatin to limit their muscle growth. And they didn't even have to lift weights! There are several naturally occurring examples of animals that don't have working myostatin proteins. Belgian Blue bulls look like competitors in the bovine version of a Mr. Universe contest. The mutation pops up fairly frequently in Whippets, a dog breed that is normally thin as, well, a whip. Whippets with the mutation look like pumped-up pit bulls with tiny heads. In recent years, scientists have identified the mutation in a couple of super-strong children.

While tinkering with the gene that codes for myostatin could prove useful in treating people with certain diseases that affect the muscles, it might not be a great idea in normal, healthy people. One of the side effects of the mutation in the Schwarzenegger mice is that their tendons—those bands of dense tissue that connect muscles to bones—become small and brittle, which would likely lead to increased injuries.

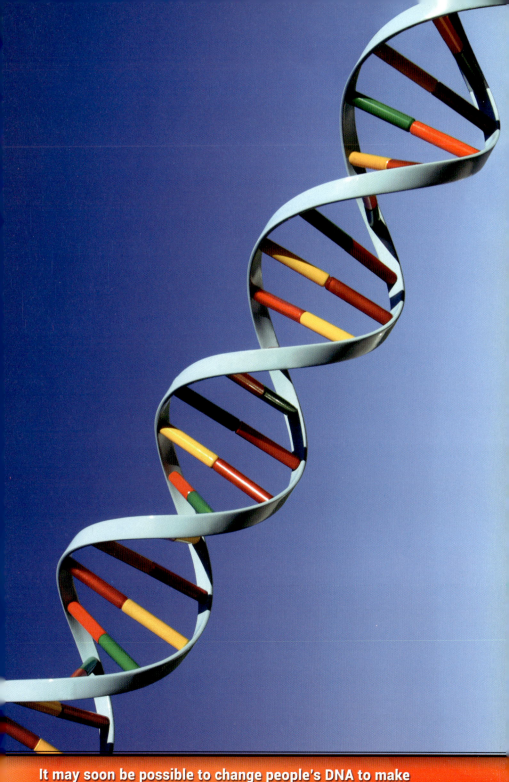

It may soon be possible to change people's DNA to make them bigger and stronger. This illustration shows the double-helix construction of DNA.

INVESTIGATE STEROIDS AND
PERFORMANCE DRUGS

PEDs Today

Clearly, athletes will go to great lengths to be faster, stronger, and tougher than their opponents—even if it means risking their careers, their health, or even their lives. In the coming chapters, we'll take a closer look at the big three classes of PEDs—amphetamines, anabolic steroids, and blood-doping products—as well as some of the methods that athletes use to cover up their illegal drug use. We'll also explore some of the nutritional supplements available. Some are legal, but many experts worry about their safety.

Chapter 3

MUSCLE BUILDERS: Anabolic Androgenic Steroids, Steroid Precursors, and Other Hormones

In 2003, seventeen-year-old Dionne Passacantando bought anabolic steroids from a boy on her high school football team. In that football-crazy town, just eleven miles away from Taylor Hooton's hometown of Plano, it was probably easier for a teenager with the available funds to buy steroids than beer. Passacantando, a cheerleader and gymnast, didn't buy the steroids because she wanted to become stronger. She wanted to look good, maybe develop an awesome six-pack. She had heard this particular form of anabolic steroid, Winstrol, could make her lean and toned.

She injected herself with the drug every other day for five weeks. She did not develop a six-pack, but she did gain ten pounds of muscle. Her voice deepened, and she developed acne on her back. She found that little things would send

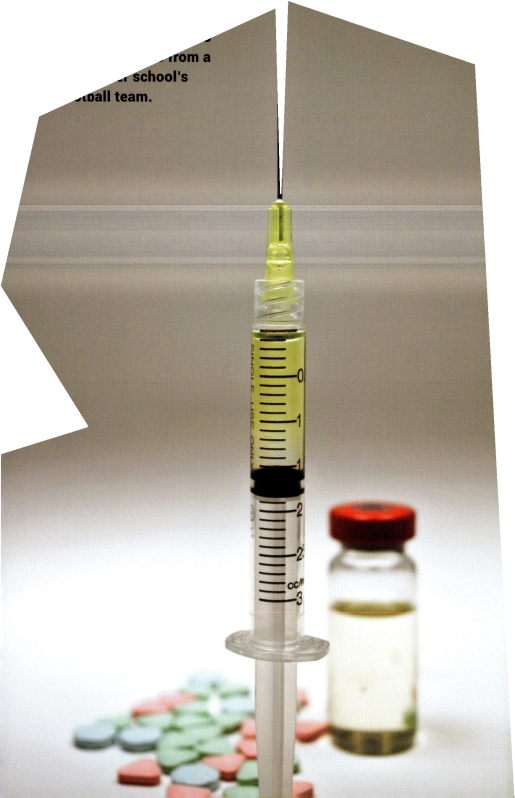

her into the "roid rage" associated with steroid use. She became depressed—so depressed, in fact, that she tried to kill herself.

Passacantando recovered, but she wants teens to understand the risks. "I didn't know anything about it," she told a *New York Times* reporter. "I didn't realize how dangerous it was or any of the side effects. It's horrible, the physical and psychological side effects, for guys and girls."[1]

Androgenic Anabolic Steroids

In men, the naturally occurring hormone testosterone is made mainly in the testes, as well as the adrenal glands. It may come as a surprise that women make small amounts of testosterone, too. The ovaries and the adrenal gland produce about one-tenth the amount that men make. Some of that gets converted into estrogen—the female hormone—while the rest is important for bone strength and keeping muscles lean and strong. Each person has a "normal" level of testosterone, which can change over a lifetime or even throughout the day. In both men and women, the pituitary gland is responsible for regulating the production of testosterone. Much like a thermostat that controls the heat in a house, the pituitary gland senses the body's testosterone levels and tweaks the levels up or down.

The testosterone molecule is carried through the bloodstream and is transported inside various kinds of cells. It attaches itself to a special receptor inside the cell, rather like a key fitting into its lock. Then the complex binds to part of the DNA molecule. In muscle cells, this triggers the

Steroids can be made into pills, liquids, gels, or creams. Liquid steroids are injected into the body.

production of protein used to make more muscle cells. It boosts hunger and the production of red blood cells. It helps the body burn fatty tissue. Other types of cells respond by making proteins that lead to increased hair growth or a deeper voice.

Most of the anabolic steroids in use today are made in the lab, "designer" versions of the naturally occurring hormone testosterone. The many types of anabolic steroids are basically variations on the four-ring testosterone molecule. By making small changes to the side chains on the molecule, chemists can subtly alter the way the steroid acts in the body. Some are so closely related to natural testosterone that they are nearly impossible to detect using standard drug testing. (These are also some of the most dangerous synthetic steroids.) Some steroids are cleared from the body

MUSCLE BUILDERS: *ANABOLIC ANDROGENIC STEROIDS, STEROID PRECURSORS, AND OTHER HORMONES*

fairly quickly, lasting only three to four weeks, a feature that makes them popular with athletes who know that they must undergo a drug test before a specific event. Others stay in the body for a long time. Depending on the type of steroids, they come in the form of pills, liquids, gels, and creams. Users typically swallow them, rub them on their skin, or inject them into their muscles. People who abuse steroids may take one to one hundred times the doses recommended for treating medical conditions, often while taking two or more types of steroids at the same time—a practice known as "stacking." It is also common for abusers to take steroids in 6- to 16-week cycles. During the "on" cycle, they take high doses, or slowly increase the dose until they reach the peak amount mid-cycle, and then taper down to the end of the cycle—also known as "pyramiding." After the cycle is finished, they stop taking the drug for a period of time

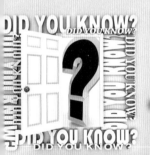

SYNTHETIC *Cortisone*

There are many other naturally occurring steroids, including the female sex hormone progesterone. Synthetic versions of cortisone, which is made in the adrenal gland, is commonly used to treat the pain and inflammation that come with sports injuries, arthritis, and asthma. While cortisone is not considered a performance-enhancing drug, its use is banned during many sporting events unless the athlete gets special permission from a doctor. These steroids do not build muscle or enhance masculine characteristics.

INVESTIGATE STEROIDS AND
PERFORMANCE DRUGS

before starting a new one. Many users believe this is a safer way to use steroids, although there is no scientific evidence to back up this belief.[2]

Steroid Alternatives

Steroids aren't the only drugs abused in the quest for bigger, stronger muscles. Human growth hormone (hGH) is a natural substance made by the pituitary gland, a pea-sized organ at the base of the brain. The hormone stimulates growth in children and teens, and increases muscle mass in adults. Synthetic hGH can be a valuable drug to treat dwarfism and a number of other conditions. It is illegal to use synthetic hGH without a prescription. Even so, athletes seeking to reduce body fat and increase lean body mass have been using hGH in increasing numbers—in part because it is so difficult to detect in drug tests. There's little evidence that hGH increases performance, but some studies indicate that it may help athletes recover from injuries. There are some sports doctors who argue that injured athletes should be allowed to use hGH under a doctor's supervision.[3] For the time being, however, hGH remains a banned substance.

If you have asthma, you may use an inhaler that delivers a drug called a beta-2 agonist, which helps relax the airways. But when it is injected into the bloodstream, the drug is believed to build muscle mass and reduce body fat. Insulin, a hormone that is produced in the pancreas, helps the body use or store the blood glucose it gets from food. People whose bodies do not make insulin or do not use insulin properly often have to take insulin shots. What many people don't know is that insulin also helps build muscle,

Some inhalers to treat asthma deliver a drug called a beta-2 agonist. This drug can be misused and injected in the bloodstream to increase muscle mass.

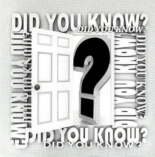

INJURIES and hGH

In 2007, Yankees pitcher Andy Pettitte was among 85 baseball players named in an investigation into steroids and performance-enhancing drugs. He admitted to using hGH in 2002 to recover from an elbow injury while on the disabled list. "I had heard that human growth hormone could promote faster healing for my elbow," he said in a statement released to the Associated Press. "I felt an obligation to get back to my team as soon as possible. For this reason, and only this reason, for two days I tried human growth hormone. Though it was not against baseball rules [hGH was not banned from baseball until 2005], I was not comfortable with what I was doing, so I stopped. . . . I wasn't looking for an edge. I was looking to heal. I have the utmost respect for baseball and have always tried to live my life in a way that would be honorable." Pettitte was not linked to steroids in the investigation, and the Yankees stood behind the pitcher.[4]

Andy Pettitte, shown here during the 2009 season, admitted to taking hGH to treat his injury seven years earlier. Although hGH was not illegal until 2005, Pettitte did not feel comfortable with the drug and stopped after two days.

which has led some athletes to abuse the hormone and a similar substance called insulin-like growth factor. Some runners also abuse insulin, because it boosts the body's supply of glycogen, a form of glucose that the muscles use for fuel. Athletes who can prove that they have asthma or diabetes are allowed to use these substances, but otherwise they are banned.

Some steroid abusers use a natural hormone called human chorionic gonadotropin (hCG) in combination with steroids. Women produce the hormone when they are pregnant. It instructs the body to produce extra testosterone. Men use hCG to restore the normal testosterone production that shuts down when they are taking steroids. It comes at a hefty price, however—it must be extracted from the urine of pregnant women.

How They Affect the Body

Steroids and related drugs do indeed increase lean muscle mass and strength, if an athlete is also willing to really hit the weights or do other training, and eats plenty of protein. A couch potato on a diet of sugary soda and chips can't take steroids and expect to look like the cartoon character the Hulk. While they may make you temporarily stronger, faster, or leaner, these drugs do not make you healthier. Steroid abusers pay a high price, not just because they are expensive (and they are) but because they also have serious side effects. Some of them never go away. To make matters worse, steroids can become addictive. Steroid users who stop

INVESTIGATE STEROIDS AND PERFORMANCE DRUGS

taking the drugs often experience withdrawal symptoms. Mood swings, fatigue, restlessness, and depression are all common.

Side effects of steroid abuse include severe acne (especially on the back), oily skin and hair, puffy cheeks, and bad breath. But these are minor in comparison with the more serious side effects. Steroid use can increase the risk of developing cancer, as well as heart, kidney, and liver disease. People who inject steroids and share needles with others are at risk for HIV (human immunodeficiency virus, the virus that causes AIDS) and liver-damaging hepatitis infections.

Steroid abuse can cause some serious psychological problems. Some people become aggressive, angry, or violent—a side effect commonly known as "roid rage." Although some steroid users, especially those in the bodybuilding community, claim that concerns over roid rage are overstated, there have been a number of murders and other violent attacks related to steroid abuse. Clinical studies have found that the people most likely to experience roid rage tended to be angry or hostile even before using steroids. However, sometimes people with no history of known violence or aggression can become this way. The drugs, experts believe, make people less able to control their emotions. So, for example, what might have been an angry exchange of words before steroid use becomes a fistfight under the influence of steroids. Long-term steroid use, as well as quitting steroids, can lead to depression and suicide.

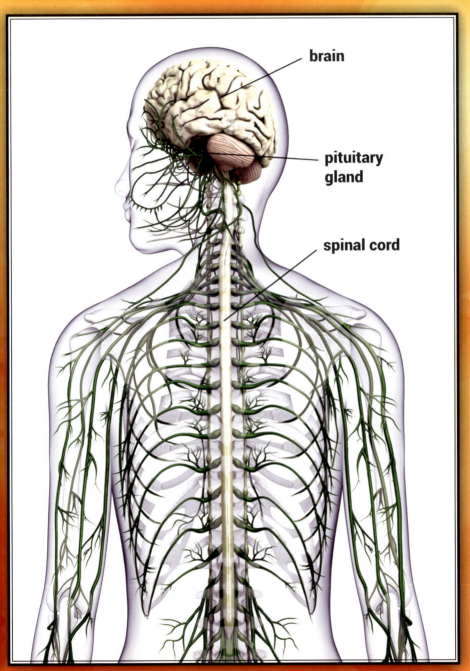

The pituitary gland, a pea-sized gland at the base of the brain, regulates the production of testosterone.

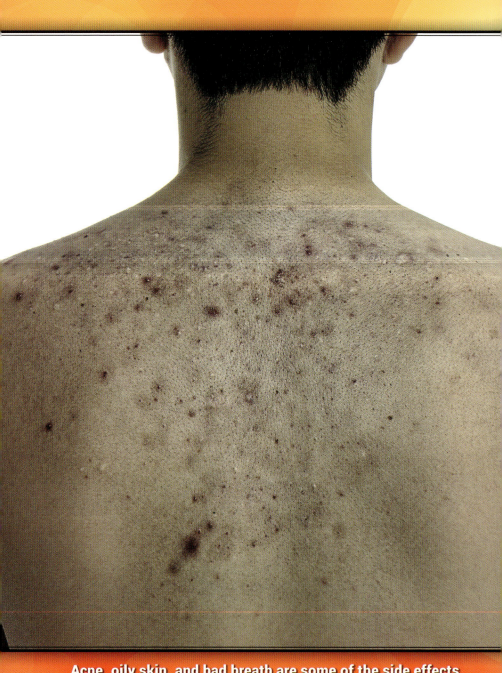

Acne, oily skin, and bad breath are some of the side effects of steroid use.

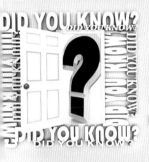

IT'S A
Scandal!

On September 24, 1988, Canadian sprinter Ben Johnson settled into his blocks at the starting line of the 100 meters final at the Seoul Olympics. A TV commentator called it "possibly the greatest field assembled for the finals of the Olympics," including former world record holder Calvin Smith and future gold medalist Linford Christie.[5] But the world was most interested in the matchup between Johnson and his bitter rival Carl Lewis, an American sprinter and reigning Olympic champion.

Bang! Johnson was first out of the blocks, sprinting with tremendous power. A mere 9.7 seconds later, the race was over. Johnson set a new world record to claim the gold medal. Lewis came in second, just over two-tenths of a second later. Sports fans were still buzzing about the exciting race two days later when officials announced that Johnson had tested positive for anabolic steroids. Johnson was stripped of his gold medal and returned to Canada in disgrace.

Even though Johnson later admitted that he had used steroids for seven years, he still claims that someone must have spiked his drink with some steroid just before his drug test. He said that he had stopped taking steroids long enough for them to clear from his system, and that he hadn't been taking the particular type of steroid they found in his urine sample. Sports fans may never know the truth, but one disturbing fact stands out: Of the eight men in that race, only two never tested positive for performance-enhancing drugs at any time in their careers.

INVESTIGATE STEROIDS AND
PERFORMANCE DRUGS

When guys take steroids, their bodies react to the overload of testosterone by producing estrogen. One result of this increase in estrogen is the development of breasts—not a great look for men. In some cases, the condition is permanent, even if the user stops taking steroids. The body also responds to the increase in testosterone by making less of it. Most testosterone is made in the testicles, and as a result, they shrink—sometimes permanently. Urinating may become painful, and some guys find that they can no longer get an erection. Long-term steroid use can even cause sterility.

Girls who take steroids can expect to see more facial hair, a deepening voice, and smaller breasts. They may lose some hair on their heads, like balding men. Some women find that their clitoris grows larger, sometimes so much that it resembles a small penis. Their menstrual cycles are often disrupted. Damage to the ovaries can cause infertility. Women who do become pregnant after steroid use are at a higher risk of having miscarriages or delivering babies with birth defects. Most of these side effects are permanent, even after stopping the steroids.

Steroids pose special dangers for teens, whose bodies and brains are still developing. Their bones stop growing, resulting in stunted growth.

Human growth hormone can cause nerve, muscle, or joint pain. It can also increase the risk of diabetes, heart disease, and an overgrowth of bones in the hands, feet, and face. And anything labeled "human growth hormone" that is not prescribed by a doctor could be just about anything. Many Web sites claim to sell "growth hormones," but

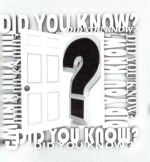

BIGOREXIA

Some people—especially boys and men—look in the mirror and see a scrawny, frail body, even if they have good muscle mass. They have a disorder that is in many ways the opposite of anorexia nervosa, in which people think they look fat even though they may be dangerously thin. People who have this disorder, sometimes called "bigorexia," obsess about their muscles. They exercise and lift weights compulsively, even to the point where they injure themselves, and often abuse steroids.

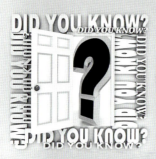

A STEROID BY ANY OTHER NAME...
...is still a steroid.

Some of the most commonly abused steroids include Deca-Durabolin®, Durabolin®, Equipoise®, and Winstrol®. You might be more likely to hear these street names:

- Pumpers
- Gym Candy
- Roids
- Arnolds (as in Arnold Schwarzenegger)
- Juice
- Sauce

chances are they are not the real thing. And if you think that hGH is worth the risk, you'd better be willing to pony up the cash: $5,000 or more each month.

The abuse of beta-2 adrenergic agonists, the asthma drugs, may lead to a too-rapid heartbeat, nausea, headaches, and dizziness. The abuse of insulin and insulin-like growth factors can be particularly dangerous. Too much insulin in the body can cause blood sugar levels to crash, leading to a coma or even death. In 2003, a former Miss Universe contestant from Scotland, Louise Nuttall-Halliwell, died after spending nearly two years in an insulin-induced coma.

If you or someone you know is abusing steroids or related muscle-building drugs, it's important to get help. Stopping the drugs cold turkey can be dangerous. It's well known that users who stop using steroids often become depressed or suicidal. This is partly due to the fact the hormones can do a number on the brain chemicals that affect the sense of well-being. But some people also base an unreasonable amount of their self-esteem on the way their chiseled, cut body looks in the mirror—despite the fact that the steroids may ruin their health. For them, it is important to accept the body that genetics handed them. With the right diet and exercise, it's possible to build a strong, healthy body without drugs.

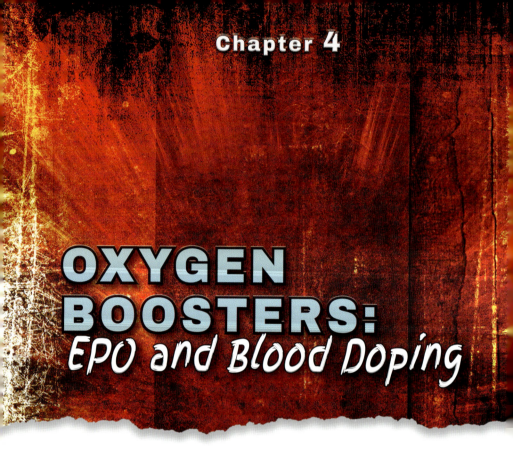

Chapter 4

OXYGEN BOOSTERS: EPO and Blood Doping

From 1999 to 2005, Lance Armstrong was at the top of the very competitive world of professional cycling. During those years, he won the grueling 21-day, 2,000-mile Tour de France bicycle race seven times in a row. His achievements seemed even more impressive in light of the fact that he had been diagnosed with cancer in 1996. At one point, doctors gave him a 40 percent chance of surviving. He beat the odds and returned to competitive cycling, stronger and faster than ever before.

But from the beginning of Armstrong's remarkable comeback, rumors began to swirl around the athlete's use of performance-enhancing drugs. Despite his repeated denials, the accusations mounted. In 2012, the U.S. Anti-Doping Agency (USADA) released a report containing evidence that Armstrong had used steroids, erythropoietin, and blood doping while competing. Former teammates who admitted to using PEDs told the USADA the techniques that they used to beat the drug tests. Not only did Armstrong use PEDs, the report said, but he also supplied banned substances to his teammates and threatened to replace those who refused to use them.[1] He bullied and attacked fellow cyclists who criticized him.

The International Cycling Union took away Armstrong's seven Tour de France titles. He was banned from competing in any sport that follows the World Anti-Doping Agency code, including cycling. Nike and other companies that paid him millions of dollars to represent their brands dropped him. The U.S. Postal Service and other companies that sponsored the team have demanded that he pay back the millions of dollars they gave him.

After years of denying the doping charges, Armstrong did an interview with Oprah Winfrey in 2013 and confessed that he had used PEDs throughout most of his cycling career. He admitted to using erythropoietin, human growth hormone, and steroids and to receiving oxygen-boosting blood transfusions. He claimed that doping was rampant in the cycling world, and that he did what he had to do to win. In the end, the doping that helped him win seven Tour de France titles destroyed his reputation, his livelihood, and possibly, his fortune.

Blood Boosting

A protein called hemoglobin in red blood cells carries oxygen from the lungs throughout the body. Muscles that are working hard—say, leg muscles powering a cyclist up a

INVESTIGATE STEROIDS AND
PERFORMANCE DRUGS

steep hill—need much more oxygen than they do while the body is at rest. It stands to reason that the more oxygen the blood cells can deliver to the muscles, the better the athlete will perform.

In the 1970s and 1980s, some athletes discovered a clever way of boosting their red blood cell counts. They would remove some of their own blood, store it, and wait a few weeks until their bodies replaced the red blood cells. Then, before an event, they put the stored red blood cells

Lance Armstrong (background) rides at L'Alpe d'Huez during stage 10 of the 2001 Tour de France.

back into their body. In some instances, athletes used someone else's blood who had the same blood type. From a cheater's point of view, blood doping had the advantage of being difficult to detect in drug tests. "Normal" levels of red blood cells vary from person to person, so who could say that they had abnormally high levels?

A scandal erupted following the 1984 Los Angeles Olympics, when it became known that one-third of the U.S. Cycling team had received blood transfusions. Three of the eight cyclists who boosted became quite ill and didn't perform well, probably because they received blood types that did not match their own. Five of the cyclists went on to win medals, though. The Olympic rules about blood boosting were unclear at the time. Still, it was widely accepted that the practice, if not illegal, was certainly not ethical. Cartoons depicting cyclists as vampires or competing with bags of blood attached to their cycles tickled the public's funny bone while criticizing the practice. The U.S. Olympic Committee banned blood boosting in 1985, and the International Olympic Committee banned it a year later.

Scientists have developed a method to test for blood transfusions from another donor, but until recently, it has been impossible to detect blood doping using the athlete's own blood. Now, scientists believe that they may be able to use a test that detects signs of aging in the red blood cells. Scientists are also developing another test that detects chemicals that come from the plastic bags in which the blood is stored.[2]

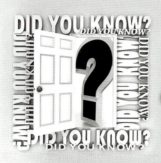

WIN at Any Cost

"For two years, I took EPO, growth hormone, anabolic steroids, testosterone, amphetamine. Just about everything. That was part of the job." — Erwan Mentheour, cyclist.

There is no doubt that many athletes feel a great deal of pressure to use performance-enhancing drugs—at any cost. The stakes are high, from the high school athlete hoping to get a football scholarship to Olympic athletes who stand to gain thousands or even millions of dollars from corporate sponsors if they win.

Consider this scenario: You are offered a banned performance-enhancing drug, with two guarantees—you will not be caught, and you will win. Would you take the drug? Sports medicine researcher Robert Goldman asked this question of elite athletes, including sprinters, powerlifters, and swimmers in 1995. Just three out of 198 athletes said no. Goldman then posed a second scenario to those same athletes: Suppose you are offered a banned performance-enhancing drug that comes with three guarantees—you will not be caught, you will win every competition that you enter for the next five years, and then you will die from side effects of the drug. Would you take it? Astonishingly, more than half the athletes said yes. Goldman had been posing those questions to elite athletes every other year since 1982, with more or less the same response every year.[7]

If a new study is accurate, attitudes may be changing. In 2012, researchers posed the same question to participants in an elite-level track and field event in North America. Roughly 12% of the athletes said that if they could take an illegal drug that would guarantee a gold medal without getting caught, they'd do so. But just two out of 212 athletes (roughly 1%) said that they'd take the drug, even they knew it would kill them after five years.[8]

Sporting officials hope that efforts to educate athletes about doping are changing attitudes. Max Siegel, head of the U.S.A. Track and Field organization, told *Runner's World* magazine ,"...Our athletes and our sport as a whole have worked very hard the last ten years to create a culture that rejects the 'win at all costs' mentality. . . . The fight to get rid of doping and support fair play is one that we are devoted to every day, year-in and year-out."[9]

Erythropoietin

Although it was nearly impossible to detect at first, blood boosting had its problems. It was complicated and messy. There was always the risk of blood-borne infections, either from dirty needles or receiving blood from people with disease. Enter a genetically engineered form of the hormone erythropoietin (EPO), in 1989. The kidneys normally produce erythropoietin, which stimulates the production of red blood cells. EPO was a life-saving drug for people who had diseases that resulted in anemia (a shortage of red blood cells). But blood-doping athletes immediately realized that they could use EPO to cheat by boosting their red blood cell counts. Athletes soon found that EPO really did boost their performance, especially in long-distance events. Unfortunately, some found that EPO (as well as blood transfusions) could also be deadly.

Blood is basically a mixture of red and white blood cells and a watery portion called plasma. The percentage of the blood that is made up of red blood cells is called the hematocrit level. Normal hematocrit levels in men are 40 to 50% in men, and 37 to 47% in women. EPO can boost the number of red blood cells dramatically above normal levels. During races, the body (and therefore blood) can lose even more water. As a result, the blood becomes thicker than normal. The heart has to work harder than ever to pump the sludgy blood throughout the body. The thickened blood can also form clots that block blood vessels and capillaries. If the clot happens in the heart, it can cause a heart attack. In the brain, it leads to a stroke (the sudden death of brain cells due to poor blood flow). As Dr. Randy Eichner, a blood

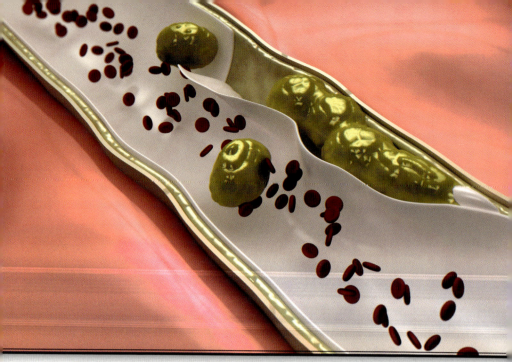

Thickened blood can form a clot (in yellow), blocking the vessel of the circulatory system.

• •

specialist at the University of Oklahoma, told the *New York Times* in 1991, "Pretty soon you have mud instead of blood; then you have trouble."[3]

In the late 1980s and early 1990s, there was a rash of deaths among European professional cyclists, all of them young and previously healthy. Although there is no proof that they were caused by EPO, experts believe that the drug was a factor in many of, if not all, the deaths. "There is no absolute proof, but there's so much smoke that most of us are convinced," Dr. Eichner stated. "You just don't get 18 deaths in 4 years, mysteriously, with 10 of them attributed to cardiac [heart] problems."[4]

One of the cyclists was Johannes Draaijer, a twenty-seven-year-old athlete from the Netherlands. He died in his sleep of a heart attack, just a few days after competing in a

OXYGEN BOOSTERS: *EPO AND BLOOD DOPING*

race in Italy. His doctor had pronounced him fit to compete before the race. His widow, Lisa Draaijer, believes that EPO caused her husband's death.[5] She hopes that his death will serve as a warning to other athletes tempted to dope.[6]

The World Anti-Doping Agency approved a reliable test for detecting genetically engineered EPO in urine samples in 2003. This test made it more difficult for athletes to

EPO is still the most widely abused drug in competitive cycling.

INVESTIGATE STEROIDS AND PERFORMANCE DRUGS

abuse the drug. This has led some athletes to go back to the old standby of blood boosting, although EPO remains the most widely used drug in competitive cycling.

Synthetic Oxygen Carriers

Ever on the lookout for new ways to boost oxygen in the blood, some athletes have turned to chemicals that have the ability to carry oxygen. Hemoglobin-like chemicals and other oxygen-carrying molecules were developed for use in emergencies where human blood is not available or there isn't enough time to find a blood type match. The serious side effects of these drugs, including an increased risk of stroke and heart attack, may be worth the risk if a patient

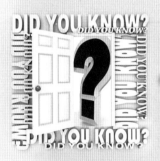

HOW TO AVOID Altitude Sickness

People who are not used to high altitudes often find that their ski vacation or hiking trip in the Rocky Mountains is ruined by something called altitude sickness. The lower levels of oxygen can cause headache, loss of appetite, dizziness, nausea, and problems with sleeping. Some people say it feels like having the flu. As the body becomes acclimated—and begins producing more red blood cells—the symptoms usually go away. Severe altitude sickness, however, can be dangerous— even fatal. It is a good idea to take it easy the first few days after traveling to a high altitude, and drink plenty of water. Better yet, try to spend a night or two at a medium altitude before going higher. If you are planning a hiking trip in the Rockies, for example, explore Denver before going higher.

High-altitude training increases the amount of red blood cells in the body.

INVESTIGATE STEROIDS AND PERFORMANCE DRUGS

is bleeding to death. But for an athlete looking to gain an edge? Not so much. As with other methods of blood doping, synthetic oxygen carriers arc banned from sporting events. Scientists developed a test to detect them in 2004.

Boosting Red Blood Cell Counts

It is possible for athletes to increase their red blood cell counts without using dangerous and illegal drugs; it's called altitude training. At high altitudes, the air is thinner. There are fewer oxygen molecules for every breath taken. The bodies of people who live in these areas make up for the thin air by making more red blood cells—we say they become acclimated. This is why athletes sometimes move to high altitudes to train. When they travel to their competitions at lower altitudes, their red blood cell count remains higher for 10 to 14 days. The high-altitude training approach has it drawbacks, though. There is the cost and expense of moving to a new place, for one thing. It is also more difficult to train hard at high altitudes. Some athletes find that at very high altitudes they begin to lose weight. Their immune systems may be less able to fight off infections. Some athletes get the same results by sleeping in a special tent that has lower-than-normal oxygen levels.

The right training techniques can also help athletes improve the body's ability to deliver and use oxygen. Regular, high-intensity workouts strengthen the heart and make it better at pumping blood, and muscles become more efficient at using the available oxygen.

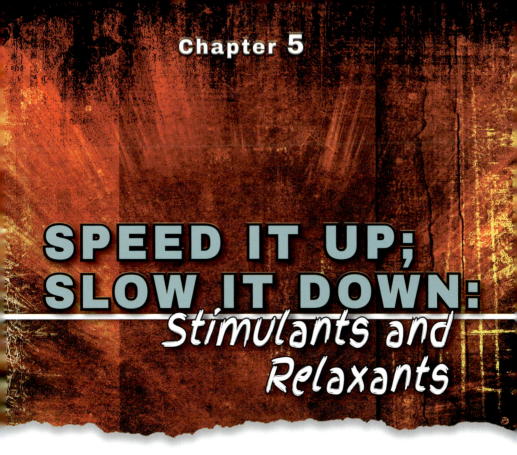

Chapter 5

SPEED IT UP; SLOW IT DOWN: Stimulants and Relaxants

Garrett Hartley, a twenty-three-year-old placekicker for the New Orleans Saints, knew that he was in for a long, sleepless night. He had to drive from Dallas to New Orleans—over seven hours—in order to make it to practice the next morning. He took a half-pill of Adderall, a prescription drug used to treat Attention Deficit Hyperactivity Disorder (ADHD). He pounded it back with a can of Red Bull. Adderall has become one of the most abused drugs among high school and college students as a "study drug." It can help calm and focus some people with ADHD by balancing out brain chemicals, but acts as a powerful stimulant for those who do not have the disorder. Hartley did not have ADHD, but he desperately needed to stay awake, so he got some from an old college buddy.

Mixing Adderall with an energy drink got NFL placekicker Garrett Hartley suspended for four games.

SPEED IT UP; SLOW IT DOWN: *STIMULANTS AND RELAXANTS*

He made it to practice, still feeling wired. A few days later, he failed a drug test. His urine contained traces of amphetamine, a major component of Adderall. Hartley, who said he didn't know that the prescription drug was banned by the NFL (unless players have a doctor's prescription for the drug), was suspended for four games.[1]

Hartley's experience marked the beginning of a growing trend of Adderall abuse in the NFL. Hartley may have used Adderall to stay awake during a long drive, but other athletes are taking it to boost their performance on the playing field. Victor Conte, the founder of the Bay Area Laboratory Co-operative infamous for supplying illegal drugs to athletes, told Fox Sports, "The players wouldn't be taking [Adderall] if they didn't think it gave them some sort of advantage. It helps with reaction time, and I know football players who have taken it. I know a lot of them."[2]

What Are Stimulants?

Stimulants are drugs that increase alertness, reduce fatigue—and, possibly, increase competitiveness. They include amphetamines (including Adderall), ephedrine (a plant-derived drug), cocaine, and caffeine. Although they all have different methods of action and side effects, they all have this in common: They act upon the central nervous system (CNS).

The central nervous system—that's the brain and the spinal cord—is the body's control center. The CNS is made up of a large network of nerves that send and receive information from other parts of the body. Each nerve, in turn, is made up of many cells called neurons. There are hundreds

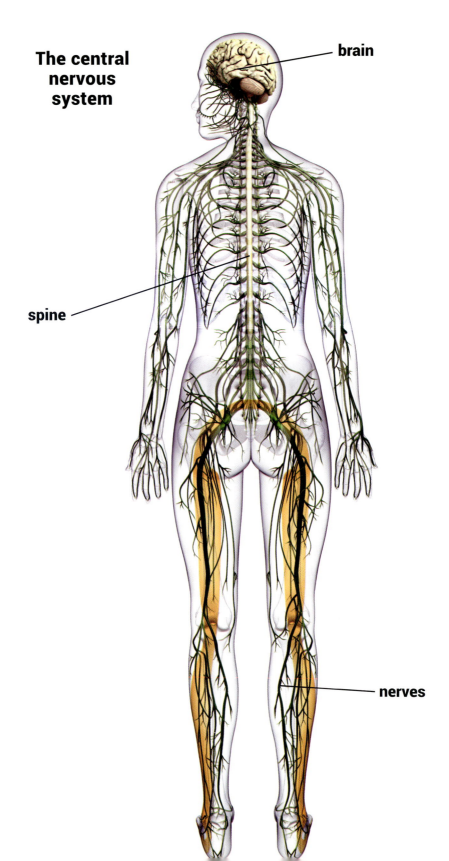

of billions of neurons in the CNS, and each one has three main parts: a cell body, dendrites, and an axon. The branch-like dendrites bring information to the cell body, and the axon passes that information along to the next neuron. The information, in the form of chemical signals called neurotransmitters, jumps from neuron to neuron across a small gap called a synapse. This process does not work properly in people with ADHD and narcolepsy (a disorder that affects the control of sleep and wakefulness). Amphetamines and other stimulants affect the actions of neurotransmitters, which is why they can help people with these disorders.

Caffeine

Chances are, you have probably taken one legal stimulant you can get without a prescription: caffeine. It is an ingredient in chocolate, coffee, tea, energy drinks, and many sodas. In moderate amounts, it's not harmful, and in fact it may even be beneficial. It gives most people a temporary energy boost and helps them concentrate better. Too much caffeine, though, can cause anxiety, dizziness, headaches, and the jitters.

Caffeine works by blocking the effects of a neurotransmitter called adenosine, a chemical that accumulates in your body during the day. Adenosine binds to receptors on nerve cells and slows down their activity. It also causes blood vessels to widen. Caffeine plays a little trick on neurons by binding to adenosine receptors, but unlike adenosine, it doesn't slow them down. Instead, the neurons speed up. A pea-sized gland in the brain senses all of this

INVESTIGATE STEROIDS AND PERFORMANCE DRUGS

commotion and decides that there must be some sort of emergency going on. It tells another gland to produce adrenaline (epinephrine)—the "fight or flight" hormone that your body produces when you see a big bully headed your way. In response, your pupils dilate, your airways open up (so that you can get more oxygen in case your muscles need it), your heart beats faster, and your blood pressure rises.

Caffeine also increases the levels of a "feel-good" neurotransmitter called dopamine. Many people say they feel happier after eating chocolate. Eating something

Caffeine is a legal stimulant. But don't overdo it; too much caffeine can cause anxiety and jitters.

that tastes delicious may have something do with it, but it is thought the caffeine in chocolate increases dopamine levels, which are associated with pleasure, movement, and attention. Some experts believe that this also contributes to the fact that many people become addicted to caffeine.

Most athletes are familiar with the benefits of caffeine—it can give an extra boost of energy during a long run, and it may decrease reaction times. In general, chugging a Red Bull or drinking a cup of coffee before an athletic event might just help, but don't over do it. Caffeine is also a diuretic, which means that it causes people to pee more often. Too much caffeine could cause an athlete to lose too much water during hot weather or long workouts. To test positive for an illegal level of caffeine at an Olympic event, you'd have to drink the equivalent of six to eight cups of coffee in one sitting.

It is important to remember that caffeine is a stimulant, and that drinking too much may be dangerous. Between 2009 and 2012, the FDA has received reports of some deaths and life-threatening conditions related to super-caffeinated energy drinks and shots. Although the reports do not prove that the products were responsible for the problems, they certainly do raise red flags.

Amphetamines, Cocaine, and Related Drugs

The stimulant that got Hartley into trouble is one of the most prescribed drugs in the U.S. Amphetamines, such as Adderall and Dexedrine, and related drugs, such as Ritalin and Concerta, help the many people who need them. The

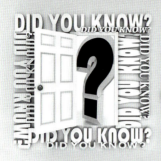

CAFFEINE: *Moderation Is the Key*

Experts say that adults should take in no more than 200 to 300 mg of caffeine a day. Teens, whose bodies and brains are still developing, should aim for no more than 100 mg of caffeine a day. Here is a list of some common products and the average amounts of caffeine they contain[4]:

Full Throttle (16 oz): 200 mg

Monster Energy Drink (16 oz): 160 mg

Starbucks Doubleshot Energy Coffee (15 oz can): 146 mg

Starbucks Frappuccino Coffee (9.5 oz bottle): 90 mg

Red Bull Energy Drink (8.3 oz): 80 mg

Mountain Dew (12 oz): 54 mg

Coca-Cola, Coke Zero, or Diet Pepsi (12 oz): 35 mg

Pepsi (12 oz): 38 mg

Pepsi MAX (12 oz): 69 mg

Snapple Lemon Tea (16 oz): 62 mg

Jolt gum (1 piece): 45 mg

Jelly Belly Extreme Sport Beans (1 oz): 50 mg

Hershey's Special Dark Chocolate Bar (1.5 oz): 20 mg

Hershey's Milk Chocolate Bar (1/6 oz): 9 mg

Zantrex-3 weight-loss supplement (2 capsules): 300 mg

Exedrin Migraine pills (2 tablets): 130 mg

NoDoz or Vivarin pills (1 caplet): 200 mg

sheer numbers of these drugs in circulation, though, mean they are also easy to buy, borrow, or steal. The result: These drugs have become one of the most commonly abused stimulants, by athletes and the general public alike. But Adderall is just one of many amphetamines that athletes—and others—have abused over the years. Cocaine, a powerful stimulant, has ruined the careers of many professional athletes.

Using amphetamines and other powerful stimulants without a prescription has been a federal crime since 1970. They can be deadly, but that hasn't stopped athletes from abusing them. Major League Baseball only banned amphetamines in 2006, after it became widely known that Major League Baseball players regularly popped "greenies" (so named for the color of the pill) to help fight fatigue and sharpen their focus over the grueling season. In 1986, Len Bias was a talented All-American basketball player; some thought he might be the next Michael Jordan. But just 48 hours after he was drafted by the Boston Celtics, he died of a cocaine overdose.

Why do athletes find these drugs so tempting? Because amphetamines suppress appetite, people sometimes take the drugs to help them lose weight. Like caffeine, amphetamines increase dopamine levels in the brain. They also increase the levels of two other neurotransmitters, serotonin and norepinephrine. These chemicals boost energy, alertness, and euphoria—that "high" feeling. Cocaine works in much the same way, and although it produces a more powerful "high," it does not last as long.

The problem with amphetamines—and to an even greater extent, cocaine—is that they can be too good at making us feel good. Abusers do not feel the need to eat or sleep; they feel they can do anything when they are using. But they can also lead to feelings of nervousness, irritability, or aggression. Abusers find it hard to sleep—even though they need the rest. They soon build tolerance to the drug—they need more and more to get that same feeling. Their bodies stop making as much of the neurotransmitters that make them feel so good. If they stop using the drug, they crash into a deep depression. They're hooked. After long-term use, stimulants can lead to high blood pressure, convulsions, heart problems, and more. Abusers may begin to see or imagine things that aren't real, or believe that others are "out to get them." Even a single high dose of an amphetamine can lead to death.

Beta Blockers

Not all athletes want that adrenaline rush when they are competing. Archers, golfers, and pool players all need steady hands and calm nerves. These are qualities that jitter-producing stimulants could never deliver. Some of them have turned to a type of drug commonly used to treat high blood pressure.

These drugs block molecules, called beta-receptors, found on certain cells in the body. This prevents stress hormones from binding to the receptors, which normally become activated when we are fearful or anxious. An archer who takes beta blockers may still feel anxious or nervous, but her hands won't tremble as she takes aim and

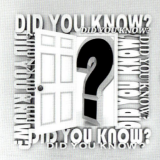

A STEROID BY ANY OTHER NAME...
...is still a stimulant.

Here is a list of some of the street names for some stimulants commonly abused by athletes:

- Crank
- Robin's Egg
- Speedball
- Disco Pellets
- Speed
- Snow
- Uppers
- Amp

lets her arrow fly. Some musicians, especially those who suffer from performance anxiety, take beta blockers before performances to help calm their nerves. It is a controversial practice among musicians, but it is not illegal.

In the sports world, on the other hand, beta blockers are considered performance-enhancing drugs. The World Anti-Doping Agency has banned their use in eighteen sports. The professional golfers organization PGA Tour banned beta blockers in 2008. That same year, at the Beijing Olympics, Kim Jong-su of North Korea had to give up his silver and bronze medals after testing positive for a beta blocker.

There is no research to show whether it is safe for healthy people to use beta blockers for long periods of time, but some musicians fear that people can become psychologically dependent upon them. "Adrenaline is increased under the strain of performances and we have to deal with it," Curtis School of Music violin professor Joseph Silverstein told the *Philadelphia Inquirer*.[3]

Chapter 6

SOMETHING ON THE SIDE:
Creatine and Other Supplements

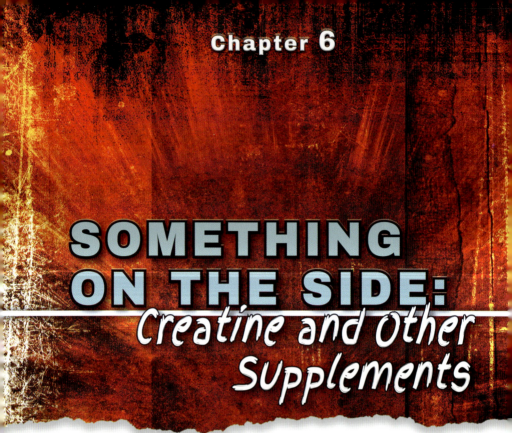

From the time Jareem Gunter was eleven years old, he dreamed of becoming a professional baseball player. In 2005, he landed a baseball scholarship at Lincoln University in Jefferson City, Missouri. People told him he had the talent to realize his dream. He began looking for legal supplements that might help him improve his performance. "I did research for three to four weeks to make sure I wasn't taking anything that could harm me," Gunter said. He settled on something called Superdrol. After taking the supplement, which had promised to boost his energy, he started feeling uncomfortable one day. "I was really lackadaisical, so I knew something was wrong," Gunter recalled. "I went home, and my eyes started turning a little yellow." He went to the hospital, and woke up the next morning with the doctor sitting by his bedside. "He told me, 'Your liver's failed. You had only a couple of days left to live if you hadn't come in.'" As it turns out, the "legal" supplement contained a potentially dangerous synthetic steroid. Not only did it nearly cost him his life; it also robbed him of his scholarship and any chance he had of playing professional baseball. Gunter recovered, and the company that made Superdrol is now out of business.

What Are Dietary Supplements?

Dietary supplements (sometimes called nutritional supplements), as defined by the FDA (Food and Drug Administration), are exactly what you might imagine: products taken by mouth that are supposed to supplement the diet. They may include vitamins and minerals, herbs or other plant materials, proteins, or the building blocks for proteins. Supplements aimed at athletes are a huge business; experts estimate that athletes in the United States alone spend nearly $4 million each year on products aimed at making them healthier or more competitive.[1] One researcher found that nearly 22% of teens surveyed took sports supplements on a regular basis; another 4.7% said that they would probably use them in the future.[2]

Critics point out that the FDA does not regulate the supplement industry. There is nothing to guarantee the purity or safety of the products. They may contain toxic ingredients or banned substances that could disqualify athletes from competitions.[3] In 2007, experts analyzed fifty-two dietary supplements sold in the United States. They found that 25% of the supplements contained traces

Store shelves are full of many types of supplements.

of anabolic steroids, and 11.5% had traces of stimulants. So what's safe, what's not, and what's just a waste of money?

Vitamins and Minerals

Nutrition experts say that most people, including teens, who eat a healthy, balanced diet get plenty of vitamins and minerals without help from pills. But what about athletes who push their bodies to the limit? Do they need a little extra help? Hard exercise increases the body's use of oxygen, which in turn produces molecules called free radicals that can be harmful to cells. Some supplements claim to help reduce the levels of free radicals, but the research supporting those claims is mixed. The verdict? Most health experts say that teens should stick to a one-a-day multivitamin.

Caffeine

Caffeine is, without a doubt, the number one supplement used today. Many popular energy drinks include caffeine, which is a stimulant. At moderate levels, it can help increase endurance, improve alertness and concentration, and enhance performance in some sports. The verdict? Caffeine is OK, in moderation.

DHEA

Dehydroepiandrosterone (DHEA) is a hormone produced by the adrenal glands. DHEA levels are naturally high in teens and young adults, but they begin to decrease by the early thirties. The body converts DHEA into both testosterone and estrogen. Some athletes take dietary supplements containing DHEA in the hopes of building more muscle

INVESTIGATE STEROIDS AND PERFORMANCE DRUGS

by boosting their testosterone levels. Makers of DHEA supplements have also marketed the product as a "fountain of youth," promising that it will slow the aging process. But recent studies have shown that DHEA does nothing to build muscle or slow the aging process. It may also increase the risk of breast cancer, prostate cancer, heart disease, diabetes, liver problems, and stroke. Since the body converts DHEA into estrogen as well as testosterone, guys who take it can expect to develop growing breasts and shrinking testicles.

Ephedra-like Products

In 2002, sixteen-year-old Sean Riggins, a wrestler and football player, bought some "Yellow Jacket" energy pills at a local convenience store. The pills, legal dietary supplements, contained caffeine and an herb called ephedra. Sometimes known by its Chinese name Ma Huang, ephedra's active ingredients are ephedrine and pseudophedrine (also found in cold medications). It is a stimulant similar to amphetamine. In traditional Chinese medicine, ephedra is used to treat asthma, colds, and other conditions. It also decreases appetite and boosts energy, which made it popular with athletes, especially those wanting to shed a few extra pounds.

The pills gave Riggins and his teammates extra energy before their wrestling meets and football games. They also gave Riggins a fatal heart attack.

The following year, Baltimore Orioles pitcher Steve Belcher died of heat stroke after taking ephedra. Riggins and Belcher were among at least 155 people whose deaths were caused by the supplement, according to the FDA. Dietary

Ephedra

supplements containing ephedra are now illegal in the United States, although it is still legal to buy and sell traditional Chinese herbal remedies containing ephedra. The National Football League, the National Collegiate Athletic Association, and the International Olympic Committee have all banned ephedra.

After ephedra-based supplements were declared illegal, "ephedra-free" products began appear on the store shelves. Manufacturers of these supplements simply replaced

INVESTIGATE STEROIDS AND PERFORMANCE DRUGS

ephedra with chemically similar compounds, such as bitter orange. There is no indication that these "ephedra-free" supplements are safe, but for now they are legal.

Protein (Whey or Casein)

Athletes trying to build muscle often try protein supplements, in the form of whey protein (a by-product of cheese making) or casein, another protein that comes from milk. Athletes may need a little more protein than the average person, because muscle fibers break down during vigorous exercise. The body uses that extra protein to rebuild the muscle—bigger and better than before. But most athletes can usually get what they need from the usual sources—milk, lean meat, fish, or protein-rich plants, such as beans—at a fraction of the cost of the supplements. Experts say that athletes need two grams of protein per kilogram of body weight. Too much protein can prompt the

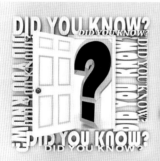

THE BANNING OF Ephedra

Not all dietary supplements are dangerous or contain illegal drugs. If you are looking for a safe supplement, look for certification from a trusted organization. Supplements carrying the blue NSF Certified for Sports logo, for example, have been tested and found to be free of potentially harmful or banned substances. There is even a NSF for Sport app to help you make informed decisions about supplements.[5]

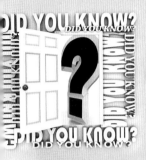

A DEATH AT THE London Marathon

In 2012, thirty-year-old Claire Squires was running the London Marathon when she collapsed in the final stretch, near Buckingham Palace. She died of cardiac arrest a short while later. Squires was running to raise funds for a charity in honor of her brother Grant, who died of a drug overdose at the age of twenty-five. Like most of the people who were taking part in the marathon, she was running for fun, not to win. She did want to beat her previous time, and so before the race she put a scoop of Jack3D, a supplement she bought on the Internet, into her water bottle. She told her boyfriend, "If I hit a bit of a wall I will take it." The supplement contained a stimulant called DMAA, which is said to boost energy and concentration. Although DMAA is not illegal, it is banned by the World Anti-Doping Agency and in competitive sports.

Doctors found high levels of DMAA in Squires's system and said that it had contributed to her death. It narrowed her blood vessels, increased blood pressure, and made her heart work too hard. It had been linked to the deaths of American soldiers doing extreme exercise, but Squires had no way of knowing that. "She innocently took a supplement which at the time was entirely legal," her boyfriend, Simon van Herrewege, told reporters. "It's clear that there needs to be far better supervision of the so-called health foods and supplements industry so that no more tragedies like this happen again."[4]

INVESTIGATE STEROIDS AND
PERFORMANCE DRUGS

body to get rid of calcium, which can result in weaker bones. That could be a real problem for teen athletes, because their bones are still forming. The verdict? Protein supplements are probably not worth it if you get plenty of protein in your regular diet. Also, too much protein is hard on the kidneys.

Creatine

Creatine, the top-selling sport supplement in the country, is a precursor of an important fuel used during short, intense exercise. Normally made in the liver, kidneys, and pancreas, it is stored in muscle tissue. Meat and fish eaters get plenty of creatine, too, but the supplement is very popular among many athletes. This is one legal , over-the-counter supplement that actually seems to deliver on its promise to increase muscle mass and strength, especially when used along with a carefully designed training program. But is it safe for teenage athletes? It's not clear. There are no studies that show it's safe to use for long periods of time, and it has not been tested in teenagers.

Creatine also has some potentially nasty side effects. Because it pulls water into the muscles, it can cause dehydration, especially for athletes working out in hot weather. It can also cause weight gain and muscle cramps. Because of these side effects, and because it has not been tested in teens, the American College of Sports Medicine does not recommend creatine for people under the age of eighteen. The verdict? If you are considering using creatine, consult your doctor first.

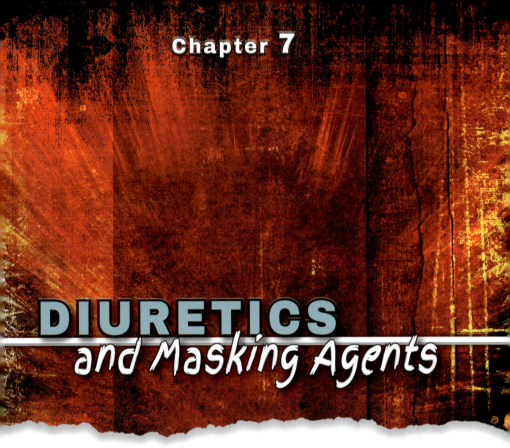

Chapter 7

DIURETICS
and Masking Agents

At age twenty-two, Jamaican sprinter Steve Mullings seemed to have a bright future. His performances in the 100-meter and 200-meter races earned him a spot on the 2004 Jamaican Olympic team. He was booted off the team, however, after a drug test found excessive levels of testosterone. He was banned from the sport for two years. He returned to competition in 2006. By 2009, he was really hitting his stride. He set a personal best in the 100 meters, becoming one of the few sprinters to break the ten-second barrier. But at the Jamaican national trials in 2011, Mullings once again tested positive for a banned drug. This time it was not for a steroid or any other type of performance-enhancing drug. Tests revealed a banned drug called

furosemide in his urine. This time, Jamaican anti-doping officials banned Mullings from athletics—for good.

Why such a harsh punishment for something that does nothing to enhance performance? Simple. Furosemide is a very effective masking agent. Masking agents are products that conceal the presence of banned substances in the urine. The only logical reason for healthy athletes to take furosemide and other masking agents is to cheat the test.

Diuretics

Furosemide is actually a type of diuretic. Most diuretics work by causing the kidneys to dump more sodium into the urine. This, in turn, pulls water from the blood and into the urine. Doctors use them to treat people with high blood pressure or other conditions where the body has too much fluid. Athletes who want to lose a lot of weight very quickly will sometimes use diuretics to lose water weight; this is a dangerous practice and is banned in most sports.

Athletes also sometimes use diuretics as masking agents because they rapidly dilute the urine. This reduces the concentration of the PEDs in the urine, making them more difficult to detect in tests. But diuretics themselves can be detected, so they are one of the many substances that drug testers screen for.

The most immediate danger posed by diuretic abuse is dehydration—sometimes severe enough to cause death. Diuretics can also cause muscle cramps, an irregular heartbeat, kidney stones, a drop in blood pressure, and heatstroke.

Jockeys often struggle to keep their weight low.

Epitestosterone

Epitestosterone is a male steroid hormone. Its structure is very similar that of testosterone, but it is not active. It has no effect on performance. In most people, the ratio of testosterone to epitestosterone is around 1:1, although in some people that ratio can be higher. Drug tests for testosterone typically measure the ratio of testosterone to epitestosterone (the T/E ratio). The World Doping Agency has ruled that a T/E ratio greater than 4:1 is evidence of doping. Athletes who abuse testosterone, then, sometimes inject themselves with epitestosterone to lower their T/E ratio. Epitestosterone itself has no known harmful side effects, but of course testosterone abuse does.

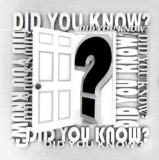

DYING TO *Lose Weight*

Some athletes use diuretics to mask their use of performance-enhancing drugs, but for others, diuretics themselves are the PEDs. Jockeys often struggle to keep their weight very low, because the lighter weight gives their horses an advantage. In the Kentucky Derby, for example, horses can carry no more than 126 pounds, including the jockey's equipment. This means that jockeys typically weigh no more than 108 to 118 pounds—in a sport that requires them to control a horse weighing well over 1,000 pounds at speeds of up to 40 mph. It is all too common for jockeys to go to drastic, and sometimes dangerous, measures to shed pounds. Some go on strict diets or force themselves to vomit after meals. Some try to lose water weight by spending time in saunas or taking diuretics. All can be very dangerous. In 2005, a twenty-two-year-old apprentice jockey named Emmanuel Jose Sanchez was found dead on the floor of the shower after riding in a race in Virginia. The official cause of death was extreme dehydration, probably the result of spending too many hours in the "sweat box," as they call the sauna, and/or taking diuretics to lose water weight.

At one time, it was also common for wrestlers, who are assigned to compete in certain weight classes, to undergo similarly drastic measures to "cut weight." At one time, wrestlers competing in NCAA events were required to weigh-in a day before the match. Wrestlers would often starve themselves, force themselves to vomit, exercise in saunas or wet suits, or take diuretics in order to shed water weight just before the weigh-in. The idea was that they could replenish their body fluids between the weigh-in and their wrestling match. But tragedy struck in 1997, when three college wrestlers died within 33 days after trying to "cut weight." This prompted the NCAA to ban the use of sweat suits, diuretics, laxatives, and sweat rooms, both on and off campus. The weigh-ins were moved from the day before the match to an hour or two before the match; athletes would no longer have time to replenish lost fluids. There were limits on how much a wrestler could lose each week.

Some wrestlers still try to "cut weight," but coaches and competitors say that it is much less common, thanks to changing rules and attitudes.

DIURETICS AND MASKING AGENTS

Probenecid

Probenecid is a drug that is normally used to treat conditions, such as gout, which is caused by too much uric acid in the blood. The drug causes the body to get rid of the excess uric acid through the urine. But it also reduces the amount of anabolic steroids passed through the urine. This drug can also be detected in the urine, so it's on the list of substances that drug testers look for.

Plasma Expanders

Plasma expanders are drugs that increase the fluid in the blood. Doctors use them to treat victims of shock, trauma, and surgery—anyone who has experienced severe blood loss. But athletes, especially those who abuse erythropoietin, use these drugs to dilute the concentration of illegal PEDs in their blood. Plasma expanders, though, can cause moderate to severe allergic reactions.

Urine Switching

And then there is the time-honored method of substituting urine samples. People have come up with all sorts of schemes to smuggle "clean" urine into testing sites, from using balloons or condoms to the more elaborate and infamous "Whizzinator." But, as many urine-soaked would-be cheaters know, these methods can go seriously wrong.

Biological Passport

In many ways, the ongoing game between would-be dopers and the testers who trying to catch them seems like a never-ending game of Whack-a-Mole. As soon as sports officials come up with a new method of testing for banned

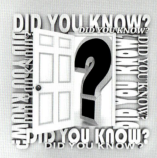

ONTERRIO SMITH and the Whizzinator

In the spring of 2005, Minnesota Vikings running back Onterrio Smith had a bit of explaining to do when authorities at the Minneapolis-St. Paul Airport found several vials of white powder in his luggage. The vials, he explained, did not contain cocaine, but dried urine. They were part of an elaborate device designed to beat drug tests. "The Original Whizzinator" consisted of a fake penis (available in a variety of skin colors), a bladder to hold the reconstituted urine (drug-free, of course), a warmer to heat the urine to body temperature, and an athletic supporter to hold the whole business together. It was a popular device with drug users hoping to pass mandatory "pee in the cup" urine tests. Smith, who had a history of substance abuse, claimed that he was bringing the device to his cousin. Later that year, he was suspended for the entire 2005 season after a third violation of the NFL's substance abuse policy. He was released from the Vikings shortly after, and hasn't played professional football since.

As for Puck Technology, the makers of the Original Whizzinator, it was found guilty of a conspiracy to defraud the government and to sell drug paraphernalia. The company is no longer in business.

substances, athletes (or their drug suppliers) come up with new ways to get around the tests. So officials at the World Anti-Doping Agency have come up with a new concept: the Athlete Biological Passport.

The biological passport is based upon the idea that each individual has his or her own "normal" levels of various biological substances. Testing officials test for biological markers from the blood and urine of professional and elite

DIURETICS *AND MASKING AGENTS*

athletes over a period of time. They compile the data to create a "normal" profile that is unique to each athlete. Any changes could point to doping. If they establish that an athlete's T/E ratio is normally 2:1, for example, a T/E ratio of 4:1 would be a definite red flag.

The governing bodies of track and field, tennis, and cycling have all adopted the biological passport program. Some experts believe that it could also be applied to the workplace to replace random drug screening.

Play Clean, Play Healthy

It can be tempting to use performance-enhancing drugs, especially when it seems like everyone else is doing it. Think twice before wasting your money on expensive, and possibly dangerous, supplements. Here are some time-tested tips for looking and doing your best:

- Get plenty of sleep. The average teenager needs more than eight hours of sleep; athletes need even more.

- Make good food choices. Focus on lean meats or other proteins, whole grains, fresh fruits and vegetables, and low-fat dairy products. These foods will not just help keep your weight in a healthy range; you'll find that they help you perform better on the playing field as well. A protein-rich snack after demanding workouts can help your body build more muscle.

- Avoid cigarettes, alcohol, and other drugs.

- If you find yourself struggling with some aspect of your sport, think about changing your training

Proper training, plenty of sleep, and a healthy diet are the safest ways to get into great athletic shape.

routine. Do you find yourself running out of fuel at the end of your races? Work to increase your cardiovascular conditioning. Would more upper-body strength help you throw the discus better? Spend more time in the weight room. Whatever you do, consult with your coach, trainer, or another trusted adult to help you design a safe training regimen.

- Learn how to relax. This may seem like a no-brainer, but relaxing doesn't always mean flopping down on the couch. A busy schedule of school, sports, and work can take a real psychological toll. Take a few minutes each day to sit quietly and focus on your breathing, do a few calming yoga poses, or visualize yourself winning that upcoming race.

Chapter Notes

Chapter 1: PERFORMANCE Drugs

1. Rebecca Leung, "The Kid Next Door," *CBS News*, December 5, 2007, <http://www.cbsnews.com/2100-500164_162-603502.html> (April 23, 2013).
2. Ibid.
3. Marla E. Eisenberg, Melanie Wall, and Dianne Neumark-Sztainer, "Muscle-Enhancing Behaviors Among Adolescent Girls and Boys," *Pediatrics*, November 19, 2012, <http://pediatrics.aappublications.org/content/early/2012/11/14/peds.2012-0095> (April 23, 2013).

Chapter 2: HISTORY OF Steroids and Performance-enhancing Drugs

1. Antonio Buti and Saul Fridman, *Drugs, Sport and the Law* (Scribblers Publishing, 2001), p. 27.
2. Charles E. Yesalis and Michael S. Bahrke, "History of Doping in Sport," *International Sports Studies*, vol. 24, no. 1, 2002, p. 45.
3. Gilbert King, "The Unknown Story of the Black Cyclone, the Cycling Champion Who Broke the Color Barrier," *Past Imperfect,* December 8, 2013, <http://blogs.smithsonianmag.com/history/2012/09/the-unknown-story-of-the-black-cyclone-the-cycling-champion-who-broke-the-color-barrier>.

4. Daniel M. Rosen, *Dope: A History of Performance Enhancement in Sports from the Nineteenth Century to Today* (Westport, Conn.: Praeger Publishers, 2008), p. 37.
5. Justin Peters, "The Man Behind the Juice," *Slate*, February 18, 2005, <http://www.slate.com/articles/sports/sports_nut/2005/02/the_man_behind_the_juice.html>.
6. Yesalis and Bahrke, p. 42.

Chapter 3
MUSCLE BUILDERS: Anabolic Androgenic Steroids, Steroid Precursors, and Other Hormones

1. Stan Grossfeld, "A Sad and Revealing Tale of Teen Steroid Use," *New York Times*, February 20, 2008, <http://www.nytimes.com/2008/02/20/sports/20iht-doping20.10225773.html?pagewanted=all> (May 10, 2013).
2. "Steroid Abuse in Today's Society: A Guide for Understanding Steroids and Related Substances," Drug Enforcement Administration, Office of Diversion Control, <http://www.deadiversion.usdoj.gov/pubs/brochures/steroids/professionals>.
3. Tom Farrey, "HGH: Performance Enhancer or Healer?" *ESPN.com*, <http://sports.espn.go.com/espn/news/story?id=2574291>.
4. "Pettitte Admits Using HGH to Recover from an Elbow Injury in 2002," <http://sports.espn.go.com/mlb/news/story?id=3156305>.
5. "30 for 30," dir. Daniel Gordon, season 2, episode 2, broadcast October 9, 2012, by ESPN Films.

Chapter 4 — OXYGEN BOOSTERS: EPO and Blood Doping

1. "Report on Proceedings Under the World Anti-Doping Code and the USADA Protocol United States Anti-Doping Agency, Claimant, v. Lance Armstrong, Respondent," *Reasoned Decision of the United States Anti-Doping Agency of Disqualification and Ineligibility,* <http://d3epuodzu3wuis.cloudfront.net/ReasonedDecision.pdf>.
2. J. Mørkeberg, "Detection of Autologous Blood Transfusions in Athletes: A Historical Perspective," *Transfusion Medicine Reviews,* 2012 Jul; 26(3):199-208. doi: 10.1016/j.tmrv.2011.09.007. Epub 2011 Nov 25.
3. Lawrence M. Fisher, "Stamina-Building Drug Linked to Athletes' Deaths," *New York Times,* May 19, 1991, <http://www.nytimes.com/1991/05/19/us/stamina-building-drug-linked-to-athletes-deaths.html?pagewanted=all&src=pm>.
4. Ibid.
5. Tom Wilkie, *Perilous Knowledge: The Human Genome Project and Its Implications* (University of California Press, 1993), p. 139.
6. Fisher.
7. Michael Bamberger and Don Yaeger, "Over the Edge," *Sports Illustrated,* April 14, 1997.
8. J. Connor, J. Woolf, and J. Mazanov, "Would They Dope? Revisiting the Goldman Dilemma," January 23, 2013, *British Journal of Sports Medicine,* pp. 697-700.
9. Amby Burfoot, "New Study Indicates Athletes Not Willing to Dope for Gold," *Runner's World,* January 23, 2013, <http://www.runnersworld.com/elite-runners/new-study-indicates-athletes-not-willing-dope-gold>.

Chapter 5
SPEED IT UP; SLOW IT DOWN: Stimulants and Relaxants

1. Mike Triplett, "New Orleans Saints Kicker Garrett Hartley Says He Took Banned Stimulant Adderall to Stay Awake," NOLA.com/*The Times-Picayune*, August 16, 2009, <http://www.nola.com/saints/index.ssf/2009/08/new_orleans_saints_kicker_garr_1.html>; Jorge Ortiz, Brent Schrotenboer, Jeff Zillgitt, "Do Pro Sports Leagues Have an Adderall Problem?" *USA Today*, <http://www.usatoday.com/story/sports/nfl/2012/11/27/adderall-in-pro-sports/1730431>.
2. A. J. Perez, "Adderall: NFL's New, Trendy PED," *Fox Sports* November 29, 2012, <http://msn.foxsports.com/nfl/story/adderall-nfls-new-trendy-ped-drug-steroids-112912>.
3. Vabren L. Watts, "Beta-blockers Used by Musicians, Athletes, Students to Enhance Performance," *Philadelphia Inquirer*, August 16, 2010, <http://articles.philly.com/2010-08-16/news/24973169_1_beta-blockers-graduate-student-performance-anxiety>.
4. Center for Science in the Public Interest, "Caffeine Content of Food & Drugs," *Nutrition Action Healthletter*, 2007, <http://www.cspinet.org/new/cafchart.htm>.

Chapter 6

SOMETHING ON THE SIDE: Creatine and Other Supplements

1. Gretchen Renyolds, "Give Us This Day our Daily Supplements," *New York Times,* March 4, 2007, <http://www.nytimes.com/2007/03/04/sports/playmagazine/04play-supplement.html?pagewanted=all>.
2. C. Roger Rees et al., "Final Report: Intermediate and High School Students' Attitudes Toward and Behavior Regarding Steroids and Sports Supplements Use: The Mediation of Clique Identity," January 30, 2007.
3. Taylor Hooton Foundation, *Dietary Supplements,* December 11, 2013, <http://taylorhooton.org/dietary-supplements/>
4. Victoria Ward, "Marathon Death: Coroner Warns of Danger of Legal Stimulants," *The Telegraph,* January 20, 2013, <http://www.telegraph.co.uk/sport/othersports/athletics/london-marathon/9837509/Marathon-death-coroner-warns-of-danger-of-legal-stimulants.html>.
5. NSF Certified by Sport, 2010, <http://www.nsfsport.com/index.asp>.

Getting Help

If you or someone you know is using steroids, a parent, school guidance counselor, or other trusted adult can help.

The national **Suicide Prevention Lifeline** (1-800-273-TALK) is a crisis hotline that can help with many mental health issues, including thoughts of suicide.

The **Substance Abuse and Mental Health Services Administration** (www.samhsa.gov/treatment, or 1-800-662-HELP) can also help people find treatment facilities, support groups, and other organizations that can provide help.

Glossary

adenosine—A neurotransmitter that slows down cell activity.

adrenal glands—A pair of organs located near the kidneys that produce the hormone adrenaline (epinephrine).

adrenaline (epinephrine)—A hormone that acts on smooth muscle, narrowing blood vessels and raising blood pressure.

amphetamine—A drug that stimulates the central nervous system.

anabolic—Muscle-building.

androgenic—Having to do with male sex characteristics, such as beard growth.

blood doping—Giving whole blood or red blood cells to an athlete.

capillaries—Tiny blood vessels connecting the small arteries and veins.

corticosteroids—Steroid hormones produced in the body or made in a laboratory. Some kinds of corticosteroids are used to treat inflammation. They do not build muscle.

creatine—A substance produced in the body or made in a laboratory. It is often taken as a supplement to increase muscle mass.

diuretics—Substances that remove water from the body.

dopamine—A neurotransmitter that is associated with feelings of well-being.

doping—The use of a substance or technique to illegally improve athletic performance.

ephedra—A dietary supplement made from a plant. It stimulates the nervous system and heart, and has been used to boost athletic performance and increase weight loss.

erythropoietin (EPO)—A hormone that stimulates the formation of red blood cells.

estrogen—A steroid hormone that promotes the growth and maintenance of the female reproductive system and female sex characteristics.

glucose—A sugar that is a source of energy for many living things.

hepatitis—Inflammation of the liver.

hormone—A substance made in the body that circulates in body fluids (such as blood) and stimulates certain cells or tissues into action.

insulin—A hormone produced by the pancreas and necessary for the normal use of glucose in the body.

neuron—A cell that is the basic working unit of the nervous system.

neurotransmitter—A substance that transmits impulses from nerve to nerve.

pituitary gland—A small organ attached to the brain that produces various hormones.

steroid—A family of chemical compounds that includes many hormones, such as estrogen and testosterone.

stroke—A sudden attack or loss of consciousness caused by a blockage of blood flow to the brain.

testosterone—A steroid hormone that stimulates the development of the male reproductive system and sex characteristics.

For More Information

Organizations

Alcoholics Anonymous
A.A. World Services, Inc.
P.O. Box 459
New York, NY 10163
(212) 870-3400
<http://www.aa.org/>

Al-Anon/Alateen
Al-Anon Family Group Headquarters
1600 Corporate Landing Parkway
Virginia Beach, VA 23454
(757) 563-1600
<http://www.al-anon.alateen.org/>

Centers for Disease Control and Prevention
1600 Clifton Road
Atlanta, GA 30333
(800) 232-4636
<http://www.cdc.gov/>

National Highway Traffic Safety Administration
1200 New Jersey Avenue, SE
West Building
Washington, DC 20590
(888) 327-4236
<http://www.nhtsa.gov/>

National Institute on Alcohol Abuse and Alcoholism (NIAAA)
Publications Distribution Center
P.O. Box 10686
Rockville, MD 20849
<http://www.niaaa.nih.gov/>

Secular Organizations for Sobriety (SOS)
4773 Hollywood Boulevard
Hollywood, CA 90027
(323) 666-4295
<http://www.cfiwest.org/sos/index.htm>

SMART Recovery
7304 Mentor Avenue, Suite F
Mentor, OH 44060
(866) 951-5357
<http://www.smartrecovery.org/>

Further Reading

Books

May, Suellen. *Steroids and Other Performance-Enhancing Drugs*. New York: Chelsea House Publications, 2011.

Roleff, Tamara L. *Performance Enhancing Drugs*. Farmington Hills, Mich.: Greenhaven Press, 2010.

Silverman, Steve. *Performance-Enhancing Drugs*. Minneapolis, Minn.: Essential Library, 2008.

Sommers, Annie Leah. *College Athletics: Steroids and Supplement Abuse*. New York: Rosen Central, 2009.

Internet Addresses

NIDA for Teens
<http://teens.drugabuse.gov>

Play Healthy: Get the Facts
<http://playhealthy.drugfree.org/facts/get-the-facts>

Index

A
Adderall, 61, 63, 67
adenosine, 65
ADHD, 11, 61, 65
adrenaline (epinephrine), 66
alcohol, 20
altitude sickness, 58
altitude training, 60
amphetamines
    abuse, 67–71
    history, 20–23
    motivations, 70
    overview, 11, 61–63
    side effects, 70–71
    testing, 63
anabolic androgenic steroids
    designer, 36–38
    mechanism of action, 35–36
    overview, 9–10
    pyramiding, 37
    side effects, 41–42, 46–49
    stacking, 37
    testing, 36–37
anorexia nervosa, 47
Armstrong, Lance, 8, 50–51
Arnold Schwarzenegger mice, 30

B
Belcher, Steve, 78–79
Belgian Blue bulls, 30
beta-2 agonists, 38, 49
beta blockers, 71–73
Bias, Len, 70
bigorexia, 47

biological passport, 87–89
blood doping
    banning, 53
    blood hematocrit levels, 54
    history, 17–20, 26–28
    mechanism of action, 51–53
    motivations, 54
    overview, 10, 50–51
    side effects, 20, 28, 29, 53
    testing, 28, 29, 53

C
caffeine, 11, 17, 65–68, 77
central nervous system (CNS), 63–65
chocolate, 66–67
cocaine, 17, 70
cortisone, synthetic, 37
creatine, 13–14, 82

D
dehydroepiandrosterone (DHEA), 77–78
depression, 6, 35, 42, 71
dietary supplements
    creatine, 13–14, 82
    ephedra, 11, 78–80
    overview, 11–14, 75–77
    side effects, 78–79, 81, 86
    vitamins and minerals, 77
    whey protein, 80–82
diuretics
    mechanism of action, 67, 84
    motivations, 84, 86
    overview, 14, 83–84
    penalties, 83–84

side effects, 84
testing, 84, 87
DMAA, 81
dopamine, 66–67
Draaijer, Johannes, 56–57

E
ephedra, 11, 78–80
ephedrine, 78
epitestosterone, 85
erythropoietin (EPO), 10, 28, 55–58
estrogen, 35, 46

F
free radicals, 77
furosemide, 83–84. *See also* diuretics

G
Galen, 15
genetic engineering, 30
Gunter, Jareem, 74–75

H
Hartley, Garrett, 61–63, 67
hemoglobin, 51, 58
Hicks, Thomas, 19
Hooton, Taylor, 5–8
House, Tom, 24
human chorionic gonadotropin (hCG), 10, 41
human growth hormone (hGH), 10, 38–41, 46–49

I
insulin-like growth factors, 10, 38–41, 49
International Olympic Committee (IOC), 21–23, 26

J
Jack3D, 81
Jensen, Knud Enemark, 20
jockeys, 86
Johnson, Ben, 26, 45

K
kola nut, 17

L
Lewis, Carl, 45
luteinizing hormone (LH), 10

M
Mullings, Steve, 83–84
muscle boosters. *See* anabolic androgenic steroids
myostatin, 30

N
narcolepsy, 65
neurotransmitters, 65–67, 71
nutritional supplements. *See* dietary supplements
Nuttall-Halliwell, Louise, 49

O
Olympic Committee, 53
Olympic Games, 15–17, 26, 28
oxygen boosters
history, 28
overview, 10, 50–51

side effects, 55–57
synthetic, 58–60
testing, 57–58

P
Passacantando, Dionne, 33–35
Pettitte, Andy, 40
pituitary gland, 35, 65–66
plasma expanders, 87
Probenecid, 87
progesterone, 37
prohormones, 10
pseudophedrine, 78

R
race horses, 29
Riggins, Sean, 78
roid rage, 35, 42

S
Sanchez, Emmanuel Jose, 86
Simpson, Tommy, 20–21
Smith, Onterrio, 88
Squires, Claire, 81
steroids
    banning of, 22–23, 26
    history, 15–17, 23–26
    muscle-building effects, 5–6
    penalties, 8, 26, 51
    side effects, 6, 8, 24, 33–35, 41–42, 46–49
    street names, 48
    testing, 26
    use demographics, 8, 26
    withdrawal, 6, 41–42, 49

stimulants
    history, 17–23
    mechanism of action, 63–67
    overview, 11, 61–63
    penalties, 73
    side effects, 19, 20, 67, 70–71, 81
    street names, 72
    testing, 63, 73
strychnine, 17, 19
suicide, 6–8, 42

T
Taylor, Major, 19
T/E ratio, 85, 89
testosterone, 9, 23–24, 35, 41, 46, 78, 85
theft, 6–8
training tips, 89–91

U
urine switching, 87, 88

W
weight loss, 14
whey protein, 80–82
Whippets, 30
Whizzinator, 88
Winstrol, 33
World Anti-Doping Agency, 26, 51, 57, 73, 88
World Weightlifting Championships, 24
wrestlers, 86

Z
Ziegler, John, 24